Biographical Sketches of Extraordinary Burpees from North America

Biographical Sketches of Extraordinary Burpees from North America

David A. Burpee

Order this book online at www.trafford.com
or email orders@trafford.com

Most Trafford titles are also available at major online book retailers.

Printed in the United States of America.

ISBN: 978-1-4669-0499-6 (sc)
ISBN: 978-1-4669-0497-2 (hc)
ISBN: 978-1-4669-0498-9 (e)

Library of Congress Control Number: 2011960898

Trafford rev. 12/09/2011

www.trafford.com

North America & International
toll-free: 1 888 232 4444 (USA & Canada)
phone: 250 383 6864 ♦ fax: 812 355 4082

Prologue

I have been very fortunate to have had the time, health and resources to complete this lengthy family research that has culminated in the biographical accounting of many extraordinary Burpees who lived in North America.

As any researcher or genealogists knows, it is sometimes nearly impossible to assure the accuracy of the information they are gathering. This certainly is the case with this book. I have attempted to list the most pertinent reference sources for each individual profiled in this manuscript. This was done to anchor my writings in the research and reports of those who came before me.

Although I have been diligent in attempting to verify the information contained within this writing, I am somewhat left to the reporting accuracy of those who have come before me. Therefore, if any errors and/or omissions have occurred within these profiles, one can only apologize in advance. The intent of this overall effort was to gather, report and preserve the varied accomplishments of these individuals who are in some way connected to each other.

As additional information on these profiled individuals, or others, becomes available it will be added to the overall information base of the Burpee family tree. Hopefully, my contribution will assist the next generation of researchers in continuing to tell the story of how the Burpee Family contributed to the history of North America.

Introduction

I believe most of us wonder if there are any famous, or infamous, distant relatives lurking in our family backgrounds. This motivation is what started my personal journey of the past thirty years in search of not only distant relatives but also family members who made substantial contributions to the fabric of their communities, states/provinces or Nation.

Over time, thousands of these relatives surfaced in my research. However, like most large groups of individuals, the vast majority of these family members were just ordinary people going about their daily lives and that is remarkable enough. They worked their jobs and tended to the welfare of their immediate families.

On occasion, I would stumble on someone who was different; someone who rose above the bar of average; someone who contributed to a cause; someone who sacrificed everything; someone who committed their life; someone who created out of nothing; or someone with great courage, tenacity and commitment to a task. These were the family members that I was most interested in pursuing and documenting through my research.

As you will see in the biographical sketches within this book, the greatness of this group of relatives spans many generations over the last four hundred years. Their actions and achievements are in varied fields of endeavor. Some displayed valor and patriotism in times of need; such as, soldiers and military officers. Others relied on their innate talents to express what they saw and felt around them; such as, artists and writers. Still others used their formal studies to build great business empires of the time; such as, business men and industrialists. While others pushed back the boundaries of the wilderness; such as, early immigrants to North America and early settlers in both New England, America and New Brunswick, Canada.

Some of the individuals in the book knew each other quite well. They were grandfathers, fathers, sons, brothers, and uncles; while other individuals in this book would have no way of making the connection to any of these family members. Although distance and time separates most of them, the commonality is their surname. They are, indeed, all family members.

I suspect most of these individuals within this book would be a bit embarrassed, if not astonished, by my characterizing them as more than just ordinary people going about their daily lives. After you have had the opportunity to read about them, and what they accomplished in their lifetimes, I think you will agree with me.

This is truly an amazing group of individuals who vastly contributed to the advancement and quality of their communities, states/provinces or Nation. They just happen to be from the same family.

David A. Burpee
November 2011

Index of Extraordinary Burpees

ANTHONY COLBY BURPEE

Born: December 16, 1817, New London, Merrimack, New Hampshire, USA

Died: October 14, 1905, New London, Merrimack, New Hampshire, USA

Burial: After October 14, 1905, Village Cemetery, New London, New Hampshire, USA

Occupation: Farmer and Merchant

Notable Accomplishments: Colonel, State New Hampshire Militia; Early College Trustee (1891), Colby-Sawyer College, New London, New Hampshire, USA

Anthony Colby Burpee was the eldest of six children born to Perley Burpee and Judith Colby. His name-sake and uncle, Anthony C. Colby, was the Governor of the State of New Hampshire in 1846 and Adjutant-General for the State of New Hampshire during the Civil War. Anthony Colby Burpee was a fourth generation resident of New London, Merrimack, New Hampshire.

"He never married but he and his sister Sarah remained on the family homestead, built 1816, with his mother, Judith. He was very musical and was a member of the choir of the Baptist Church in New London for 65 years, for 54 years of which he was the choir leader."

1

Some years ago, the following account was published in a New London newspaper:

> In the early days the voices were accompanied by the bass violin . . . later this instrument was supplemented by the piano, flute and first and second violin, it being found that the piano, would 'drown any discrepancies which might occur among the voices' . . . a little incident concerning the early days of this choir may be of interest to some. About the year 1845 it was suggested by some one that the ladies would sing much better without their bonnets, which were the large shining bonnets of these days, and as it would hardly be proper to attend church with uncovered heads a compromise was effected and small caps were substituted for the bonnets, substantial caps of lace, covering the ears and tied down under the chin. This fashion prevailed only one year. Mr. Burpee's father and grandfather sang in the choir, and at the present time three of his nieces are singing there, making the forth generation of Burpees which have sung in the New London choir, covering a continuous period of 100 years.

References:

Burpee Family, FTW, Internet Webpage

20th Century Biographical Dictionary of Notable Americans, Volume 2, Page 307.

American Genealogical-Biographical Index, Godfrey Memorial Library, 1999

Mirror to America: A History of New London, Merrimack, New Hampshire, 1900-1950, Page 361.

Federal USA Census, 1850, 1860, 1870, 1900

ASA BURPEE

Born: August 10, 1760, Rowley, Essex, Massachusetts, USA
Died: October 15, 1843, New London, Merrimack, New Hampshire, USA
Buried: After October 15, 1843, New London, Merrimack, New Hampshire, USA

Occupation: Farmer

Notable Accomplishment: Original Settler, New London, Merrimack, New Hampshire, USA

Asa married Mary Perley in Boxford, Essex, Massachusetts on November 20, 1781. During their marriage, they had nine children who became the original Burpees to populate the New London area.

Old record states:

> They came to New London from Rowley, Massachusetts, about 1786, a Shoemaker who not only intended to work at his trade in the new settlement but had grit and perseverance enough to clear a farm and establish a long enduring name in his adopted town. He pitched his camp on the southeasterly slope of the eminence now known as Burpee Hill and lived on his first location (now Miss Catherine Whittemere's) though in a new house until his death. Asa was a man of strict integrity, temperate, industrious, hospitable; was very musical, had keen wit and was as willing to take a joke as to give one. He married Mary, daughter of Benjamin and Apphia Perley of Rowley, Massachusetts, and they were the parents of three sons and six daughters. The sons inherited their father's many good qualities and the daughters were of religious habits, modest in deportment, had a great sense of propriety, were fine singers and well skilled in all kinds of handiwork from spinning and weaving to the stitching and embroidering of that date and had the ingenuity to invent new and tasteful

patterns in the latter class of work. They were economical, good managers, and best of all, good homemakers. With one exception the sons and daughters all lived and died in New London.

References:

Burpee Family, FTW, Internet Webpage

BENJAMIN PRATT BURPEE

Born: August 27, 1818, New London, Merrimack, New Hampshire, USA

Died: November 8, 1888, New London, Merrimack, New Hampshire, USA

Burial: After November 8, 1888, Pine Grove Cemetery, Lot 28-470-3 New London, Merrimack, New Hampshire, USA

Occupation: Merchant

Notable Accomplishments: Colonel, Regimental Commander, New Hampshire State Militia; Local and State Legislator, Sutton, Hopkinton and New London, New Hampshire, USA

Benjamin Pratt Burpee married Martha Jane Carr on February 21, 1855 in New London, Merrimack, New Hampshire. Mr. and Mrs. Burpee had five children (two boys and 3 girls).

The following, taken from the *Manchester Union* Newspaper of November 8, 1888, provides a background into the life of Colonel Burpee who was an active and influential citizen of Manchester, New Hampshire. He did a good share of the public work, and made many friends while there.

> The end, which had been expected for some days in the life of Colonel Benjamin P. Burpee, came at 3:10 o'clock this morning, when his spirit peacefully and without a struggle forsook its tenement of clay and soared to realms of immortality. During the middle of the past summer the first evidence of the undermining of his health became manifest, and he slowly but surely failed, until about the first of September, when he became in a large degree restricted to his pleasant residence at No. 417 Central Street, and ten days since took his bed, where he lay failing day by day, fully conscious of his approaching dissolution, and awaiting the same with calmness, and without the slightest semblance of fear.

Mr. Burpee was born in New London August 27, 1818 and was the fourth of five children born to Thomas and Lydia (Blake) Burpee. The first forty years of his life were passed in his native town, where he was educated and became a successful agriculturist.

He left there to engage in mercantile business in the neighboring town of Sutton, where he became a prominent merchant. From Sutton he removed to Hopkinton, where he was at the head of a store for a time, and purchased what is now known as the Grassmere farm, at Goffstown, where he engaged in farming. In 1871 he located in Manchester, and engaging in the grocery trade was thus actively employed for some years in the Museum building. His career in this city is well known; however, he was most known for trade in the store at the corner of Lake Avenue and Massabesic Street.

While at New London, he held every office within the gift of the town, representing the town in the legislature, and was also a member for years. At Sutton he enjoyed similar honors from his fellow-citizens, being town treasurer during the period of the war. Here in Manchester, too, he was singled out as a public servant, and served in the common council and in various other capacities. He was a candidate for the last time in ward six at the election of 1884, when he ran for representative. He was an uncompromising Democrat at all times and under all circumstances, and never lacked the courage of his convictions. He took a deep interest in the current political events of the day, was an ardent admirer of President Cleveland, and one of the last topics he spoke about was that of the approaching election.

In religion he was a Spiritualist, and was one who was never ashamed to be known as such. He was the backbone of the society in Manchester. His wife died sixteen years since, and from that time until the family ties were broken by Mr. Burpee's death he and his children have been closely allied in each other's affections. He was everything that a father could be to his family, and his strong affection was met by a current of love equally as ardent from them to him. The children are Nellie J., Harry H., Jennie A., Hattie, and William B. The first three named reside at home, while Hattie was the wife of L. H. Dyer, an attorney at Portland, Maine, and William B. resides on Young Street. One sister, Mrs. Jacob Messer, of Springfield, completes the list of immediate survivors.

There was a straightforward earnestness about Colonel Burpee's presence which ever commanded respectful attention when he was speaking, and all who have ever been thrown into his companionship were warmed into a feeling of esteem and high regard for him. He was a kind neighbor, true as the needle to the pole in his friendship, generous with his means and generous to the faults of other. Truly, a good man has been taken from the walks of life in his death, which resulted from heart disease.

His title of colonel was acquired in the old state militia, in which he won his way by promotion from ensign to the command of a regiment.

References:

Manchester Union, Newspaper, November 8, 1888
Federal USA Census, 1850, 1860, 1880
Burpee Family, FTW, Internet Webpage
American-Genealogical Biographical Index, Godfrey Memorial Library, 1908, Volume 4, Page 676.

CHARLES E. BURPEE

Born: March 3, 1853, Hooksett, Manchester, Hillsborough, New Hampshire, USA

Died: May 2, 1902, Neillsville, Clark, Wisconsin, USA

Burial: After May 2, 1902, Neillsville City Cemetery, Plot F-25, Neillsville, Clark, Wisconsin, USA

Occupation: Merchant, Farmer, Local Politician

Notable Accomplishments: Long-Term County Treasurer, Clark County, Wisconsin, USA

Mr. Charles E. Burpee married twice. He married Adelia Jones of Minerva, Essex, New York in 1877. They had two children: Charles Henry Burpee and Henry N. Burpee. After Adelia's passing on August 5, 1897, Charles married Agnes Zassenhaus of Houghton, Michigan. Charles' parents were Gain D. Burpee and Nancy Gilman. Both his parents were originally from New Brunswick, Canada. He was the third of seven children. His father was a descendant of the Puritan family of Gilmans, who came to America in the days of the Mayflower, and were among the first settlers in the New Hampshire wilderness.

> Charles E. Burpee, whose sudden death is chronicled in another column, was born at Hooksett, New Hampshire, March 4, 1853. He was the son of Gain and Nancy Burpee and came of an old New England family. In 1871 he came to Wisconsin, stopping at Oshkosh. In 1875 he came to Clark County and for a number of years followed the lumbering business, then the chief industry of this region. Later, he settled on land near Christie in the town of Weston, where he began to open up a farm. He took a great interest in farming and stock raising, being very successful in this line and at times buying and shipping stock to Chicago. His judgment in local affairs was considered excellent and for many years he was a member of the school board and as chairman of Weston, represented his town upon the county board. About two years ago he sold his farm and moved to Neillsville,

following stock buying until elected county treasurer in the fall of 1900. Mr. Burpee was a man of exemplary habits, quiet and reserved, a type of New Englander, transplanted in the broader fields of western activity. Conservative and reticent, he never attempted to gain popularity, but he was steadfast to old friends and had their sincere and hearty regards. His sudden death has cast a gloom about the court house, and the entire community looks upon his death as a calamity. In connection with the disaster which brought sudden death to another of our citizens, the sudden death of Mr. Burpee shocked and saddened the people of Neillsville and the entire county beyond description. He leaves one son, by his first wife, a young man who at the time of his father's death, was in Oregon, and who is expected home today. His wife, formerly Miss Agnes Zassenhaus, survives him, also one brother, R. Dudley Burpee of Exeter, New Hampshire, and two sisters, Mrs. Annie M. Coleman, also of Exeter, and Mrs. Maria L. White of Oakland, Cal. The funeral was held Tuesday afternoon from the Armory, under the auspices of the Free Masons, of which order he was for many years a member. Reverend T. Grafton Owen officiated.

In another newspaper report, Mr. Burpee's last moments were captured in the following article:

Never was there a lighter hearted or happier gathering of the society people of Neillsville than that which filled the big opera hall on Friday night. The Mandolin Club had finished a musical program of great excellence, and the dancing had been underway for nearly an hour, when suddenly there was a crash, dancing and music ceased, and it was seen that Mr. Burpee was lying at full length upon the floor. Owing to the extreme smoothness of the floor a number of people had in the time past fallen while dancing, and at first the only thought they had was that another accident of that kind had taken place. But instantly ready hands sought to assist him to his feet, and even those who finally raised him up were slow to comprehend the awfulness of the truth. Physicians used every means known to resuscitate him, he was then taken to this home across the street and everything done that was possible, but the end had come before he had fallen to the floor at the hall, and mournfully the throng of anxious friends who swarmed through hall and street and yard were compelled to admit and too realized that their big-hearted friend had been snatched by the hand of death from the midst of gaiety and conviviality to begin his eternal sleep.

The wife was present in the hall and participating in the dance, and although instantly at his side, and doing everything that love and her knowledge as a former trained nurse could suggest, she was last to realize the truth, and all through the night resolutely stayed at his side, hoping to see some glimmer of returning consciousness.

His death fell upon the community like a bolt of lightning from clear sky. The writer of this article had chatted with decedent but a moment before, and he was in the best of spirits, and spoke particularly of the fine time he was having. All who had talked with him make similar report of seemingly good health and high spirits.

Charles Burpee was born at Hooksett, N.H., March 4, 1853, and was therefore a little over 49 years of age. His father was G. Burpee, who was a descendant of the Puritan family of Gilmans, who came to America in the days of the Mayflower, and were among the first settlers in the New Hampshire wilderness. When a lad Charles came west, and worked at whatever came to hand at Oshkosh and vicinity, working for Pheletus Sawyer at one time. In the seventies he settled at Christie (Clark Co., Wis.), cleared up a fine time farm, and had lived there since, until he moved to Neillsville in 1899, disposing of the farm. For years he was chairman of the town of Weston, and a prominent and potent influence in county matters, acting as delegate to county, congressional and state conventions a great many times. He leaves a wife, Agnes Zassenhaus Burpee., and a son by a former marriage;

a brother, R. Dudley Burpee, and sister, Mrs. Annie L. Coleman, both of Exeter, N.H.; Also a sister, Maria L. White of Oakland, Calif.

The funeral services were held at the opera house Tuesday at 2 p.m., under Masonic auspices, T. Grafton Owen officiating. A quartet composed of Messrs. S.M. Marsh, H.C. Clark, J.A. Phillips and Gus Klopf sang. Beautiful floral tributes were tastefully arranged. The great hall was filled with grief-stricken friends who were deeply moved by the noble discourse delivered by Mr. Owen.

After the Masonic services for the dead, conducted by worthy Master S.M. Marsh, the procession moved to the cemetery, the county board and officers attending in a body and marching with the Masons. The pallbearers were: Dan Kennedy, C.A. Youmans, M.C. Ring, A.B. Marsh, H.H. Heath and Jos. Morley.

As county treasurer Mr. Burpee had been faithful and efficient, and impaired his health by his devotion to duty. In every relation of life he was square and fair, his home was one of unalloyed happiness, and he owned one of the handsomest in the city. His passing away leaves a distinct and acute sense of irreparable loss in the minds of all, whose sympathy for the bereaved wife is immeasurably great.

References:

Neillsville Time and *Clark County Republic and Press*, Neillsville, Clark, Wisconsin, published May 8, 1902
Federal Census, 1860, 1870, 1880, 1900
Wisconsin Vital Records Death Index, 1820-1907, Volume 1, Page 53.

CHARLES SIDNEY BURPEE

Birth: June 18, 1817 Sheffield, Sunbury, York, New Brunswick, Canada
Death: November 29, 1909 Sheffield, Sunbury, York, New Brunswick, Canada
Burial: After November 29, 1909 United Baptist Church, Maugerville, Sunbury, New Brunswick, Canada

Occupation: Farmer

Notable Accomplishments: Member, Provincial Board of Agriculture, 1864-1865, Sunbury Representative to the Canadian House of Commons, 1867-1887; New Brunswick Representative, Senate of Canada, 1900

The Honorable Charles Sidney Burpee was the son of Jeremiah Burpee and Elizabeth Betsey Stickney. Charles was the youngest of eleven children. Charles' father and grandfather immigrated from Rowley, Massachusetts to the Saint John River Valley around 1763. Charles was educated at the common school in Sheffield. Mr. Burpee was married three times. He had two children by his second marriage.

During the 3rd Canadian Parliament, which was in session from March 26, 1874 until August 17, 1878, both Charles and his nephew Isaac Burpee, Jr. served at the same time in this legislative body. They both represented separate jurisdictions within the province of New Brunswick, Canada.

The following obituary sketch reflects the feelings and sentiments of people at the time of his death.

> The Honorable Charles Burpee, late senator and for about a twenty years, Representative of Sunbury in the Dominion House of Commons, passed away at his residence, Sheffield at 8 o'clock Nov. 29th., [1909] aged 92 years. The funeral will take place on Wednesday at 1 p.m. The deceased, who was for years a prominent resident of Sunbury, is survived by two sons, Sydney of Sheffield, and Thomas P. of Gagetown. The late Hon. Issac Burpee was a nephew of the deceased and he was an uncle by marriage of the late Senator Wark.
>
> He was a life long liberal and represented Sunbury in the House of Commons from Confederation down to 1882 when he suffered defeat. In 1898 he was called to the senate and occupied a seat in that body for one year, at the end of the session he resigned to become Commissioner to the Paris Exposition.
>
> He was a man of kindly disposition and enjoyed the respect of all who knew him. After his retirement from the senate he continued to take an active interest in politics and held the office of President of the Queens Sunbury Liberal Association, up to the time of his death. For years the deceased carried on extensive farming operations at Sheffield and was possessed of considerable property.
>
> He married first, June 9, 1848, Mary Perley, who died December 16, 1850. Married second, March 20, 1853, to Charlotte Hayward Perley, the sister of his first wife. She died the June 19, 1861, the day after the birth of her second son, Thomas Perley Burpee. The first son, Charles Sidney was born the June 5, 1859. Married third, September 4, 1871, to Elizabeth Morrow who died February 3, 1903.

References:

Political Biography from the Library of Parliament
The Canadian parliamentary companion and annual register, 1880
The Canadian Directory of Parliament 1867-1967 by J.K. Johnson, 1968
Burpee Family, FTW, Internet Webpage
History and Genealogy of the Perley Family, Page 218.
Census of Canada, 1851, 1871, 1881
The Quiet Adventurers of North America, by Marion Turk, 2007

CHARLES WINSLOW BURPEE

Born: November 13, 1859 Rocky Hill, Hartford, Connecticut, USA
Death: May 13, 1945 Rocky Hill, Hartford, Connecticut, USA
Burial: After May 13, 1945, Grove Hill Cemetery, 22 Cemetary Avenue,
    Vernon, Rockville, Tolland, Connecticut, USA

Occupation: Editor of the *American,* Waterbury, Connecticut, 1883-1891;
    Editor of the *Standard,* Bridgeport, Connecticut, 1891-1895; Editor of
    the *Hartford Courant,* Hartford, Connecticut, 1895-1904; Department
    Head, Phoenix Mutual Life Insurance Company, 1904-1935; Literary
    Editor, *Hartford Times*, Hartford, Connecticut, 1930-1935; Author,
    History of Hartford County and *A Century in Hartford*

Notable Accomplishments: Military: First Regiment, Connecticut
    National Guard; Second Lieutenant, Company A, Second Regiment,
    Waterbury, Connecticut, USA; Adjutant, Fourth Regiment,
    Bridgeport, Connecticut, USA 1892; Captain, Company K, Fourth
    Regiment, Bridgeport, Connecticut, USA 1892; Inspector, Small
    Arms, First Regiment, Hartford, Connecticut, USA; Aide, First
    Regiment, Connecticut Volunteer Infantry, Spanish-American War;
    Colonel, First Infantry, Connecticut State Guard, World War One,
    1917-1921

Community Service: Secretary, Hartford Board of School Visitors, Hartford, Connecticut; President, Hartford Yale Alumni Association, Hartford, Connecticut

Charles Winslow Burpee's parents were Thomas Francis Burpee and Adeline Minerva Hardwood. Charles had an older brother Lucien Francis Burpee. Both brothers, in addition to their father, served in the defense of their county. All three members of this family are included in this book for their accomplishments both on and off the battlefield. Charles traced his lineage to ancestors who fought in the American Revolutionary War and, as a result, became a member of the Sons of the American Revolution.

Charles attended and graduated from Yale University in 1883 with a Bachelor of Arts degree. Following his older brother's footsteps, he is listed as a member of Yale's secret Skull and Bones society. This society is the oldest secret organization connected with Yale University having been in existence since 1832.

Mr. Burpee married Bertha Stiles of Bridgeport, Connecticut on November 5, 1885. They had one child. Stiles Burpee was born on April 12, 1903 and died in March 23, 1982 in Southbury, Connecticut. Bertha was the daughter of Ransom Stiles and Anna Stillman. She was a direct descendant of Francis Stiles of Milbroke, England, who came to Windsor, Connecticut in 1635, and whose brother was the ancestor of President Ezra Stiles of Yale College. Charles and Bertha had one child during their marriage. Stiles Burpee, a son, was born April 12, 1903.

At one point in their marriage, Mrs. Bertha Stiles Burpee found a colored lithograph of the famous Woolf portrait of Mark Twain in her house attic. She launched an effort to locate and acquire the original portrait. Based on these efforts, she was able to locate, purchase and donate the original portrait to the Mark Twain House in Hartford, Connecticut. For several decades, it was on loan to the National Portrait Gallery. In 1983, it was returned to the Mark Twain House.

Charles was a prolific writer during his adult years. A collection of his writings is housed in the Charles Winslow Burpee Collection, Manuscripts and Archives Department of the Yale University Library, New Haven,

Connecticut. The following is a sampling of his writing skills excerpted from *The Story of Connecticut*:

For many years, Colonel Charles Winslow Burpee has been a familiar figure in Connecticut life. A newspaperman and writer by training, he has become one of the contemporary historians of the State, while his military service, his business connections and public interests around the State have enhanced the scope of his influence.

Colonel Burpee was born in Rockville, Tolland County, on November 13, 1859, son of Thomas F and Adeline M (Harwood) Burpee. He is descended from old Colonial stock on both sides of his family, and in the paternal line traces his ancestry in the seventh generation from Thomas Burpee, who came to this country from England. Colonel Burpee's father, Thomas Francis Burpee, was a woolen manufacturer in Rockville, Connecticut. An officer of the old State militia, he raised one of the first companies in response to Lincoln's call for volunteers in 1861, and afterward raised another, which went out with the Fourteenth Connecticut Volunteers. At the special request of Governor Buckingham, he accepted a commission as Lieutenant-Colonel in the Twenty-first Connecticut Volunteers, of which he became Colonel and served until he was mortally wounded at Cold Harbor on June 9, 1864. Both of his sons inherited his interest in military affairs. The elder, Lucien Francis Burpee, Yale '79, during some twenty-five years of service in the Connecticut National Guard, rose to the rank of colonel and served as such in the Spanish-American War, chiefly on the staff of General Wilson, in Cuba and Porto Rico. Afterward, during the World War, he was called upon to head the Connecticut State Guard of five regiments and auxiliaries, as president of the Military Emergency Board and to sit as a member of the Council of Defense. In these connections, at the suggestion of the War Department, he accepted the appointment of major-general. In civil life he was a lawyer and his career, marked in earlier judicial service, culminated with his appointment to the

Connecticut Supreme Court in 1921. On this bench he served until his death, May 9, 1924.

Charles Winslow Burpee, younger son of Thomas F and Adeline M. (Harwood) Burpee, received his early education in the public schools of Rockville, where he finished the high school course. He was graduated at Yale in 1883. While he was still in high school he established a school publication, and after he entered Yale he became a member of the staff of the *Yale Daily News* and was its chairman in 1880. Following his graduation he turned naturally to a newspaper career, and from 1883 to 1891 served as city editor of the Waterbury *American*. From 1891 to 1895, he was associate editor of the Bridgeport *Standard,* and in the latter year joined the staff of the Hartford *Courant*. His subsequent activities have centered largely in this city. He remained with the Hartford *Courant* for nine years and, from 1900 to 1904, was its managing editor. He resigned to become associated with the Phoenix Mutual Life Insurance Company, of Hartford, as editor, and continued with this organization in other capacities through some three decades. At the time of his retirement, in 1935, he was in charge of the reinstatement division.

During the intervening years, Colonel Burpee continuued his literary interests. He wrote a number of short stories and contributed articles to various periodicals. These were chiefly on historical subjects. He is the author of *The Military History of Waterbury,* 1896; *History of Hartford County,* 1928; *A Century of Hartford,* 1931; *Connecticut in Colonial Wars* 1933; and *The Story of Connecticut, Constitution State,* 1937. He was a contributor of Dr. Anderson's early *History of Waterbury,* 1896, and the *History of Connecticut* published in monograph form, in 1925, and is author of the present work. In 1930, Colonel Burpee also returned to newspaper work as literary editor of the *Hartford Times* and served as such, in addition to his other duties until 1935.

Colonel Burpee's military career also covers an extended period. On five different occasions and in three different regiments he has held commissions in the Connecticut National Guard. During the Spanish-American War, although his service had terminated the previous year, he joined the staff of Colonel Charles L. Burdett, First Infantry, without commission, and returned when it appeared there would be no field activity. The World War found him beyond the age limit for active service, but he volunteered in other capacities and was assigned as district commander and colonel of the First Infantry, Connecticut State Guard, continuing as such from 1917 until the disbandment of these troops in 1921. The State Guard was composed of men not called into the National Army because of age or other exemption and had for its duties the guarding of munitions plants and other vital industries as well as general protective service within the State and under State control.

Colonel Burpee has taken an active interest in civic as well as military affairs, and in his own community has served as a member of the Board of Education, the High School Building Committee, and as secretary of the Municipal Art Society, of Hartford. He is a member of the Connecticut Historical Society, the Sons of the American Revolution, the national council of the National Economic League, and the National Citizen's League for Sound Banking, of which he was for a time State Secretary in Connecticut. At Yale he became a member of Skull and Bones and of the Gamma Nu and PSA Upsilon fraternities. He has always continued his interest in the University and has served s president of the Hartford County Yale Alumni Association, and as secretary of the Hartford Yale Loan Fund. In addition to these connections Colonel Burpee is a member of the Twilight Club, of Hartford, and of several honorary military organizations, including the Twenty-first Regiment, Connecticut Volunteers Association, of which he is past president. He is a Republican in politics, and a member of the Congregational Church.

On November 5, 1885, Colonel Burpee married Bertha Stiles, daughter of Ransom B. and Anna (Stillman) Stiles, of Bridgeport. They have one son, Stiles, a graduate of Yale in the class of 1926, and recently a member of the staff of the *Hartford Times*.

References:

Hartford Courant Magazine, November 23, 1947

Genealogical and Family History of the State of Connecticut, Vol. I-IV

Index of Connecticut Muster Roll for the Spanish-American War 1898-1904, Page 27.

Record of Service of Connecticut Men In the Army, Navy & Marine Corps of the United States in the Spanish-American War, Phillipine Insurrection, and China Relief Expedition from April 21, 1898 to July 4, 1904, Compiled by Authority of General Assembly under direction of Adjutant General, State of Connecticut

The Story of Connecticut by Charles Winslow Burpee, Pages 96-97.

The Military History of Waterbury by Charles Winslow Burpee

Wikipedia, Intenet Webpage

CLARENCE LAMAR BURPEE

Born: September 12, 1894 Jackson, Butts, Georgia, USA
Died: October 4, 1956 Jacksonville, Duval, Florida, USA
Buried: After October 6, 1956, Evergreen Cemetery, Jacksonville, Duval,
Florida, USA

Occupation: Railroad and Transportation Supervisor, Jacksonville,
Florida, USA

Notable Accomplishment: Brigadier General, US Army, European
Theatre, World War II

Clarence Lamar Burpee was the second of four children born to James
Arthur Burpee and Katherine Milledge Smith. His father died when he
was only eight years old. His mother remarried after the passing of his
father. Clarence never married dedicating himself to his Country and its
military service.

There is little known information about him outside of his military service.
Clarence Burpee registered to join the United States Marine Corp on July
4, 1918. By September 25, 1918, he is reported to have been in France to
fight in World War One. He continues to be assigned in France through
August 13, 1919. On January 8, 1919, he is promoted from private to
corporal.

Prior to his enlistment in World War II, he was the Superintendent of
Terminals, Atlantic Coastal Lines located in Jacksonville, Florida. This
railroad terminal was, at the time, the largest such facility in the South.

In fact, many of the officers who were later affiliated with him in Europe were fellow employees of this railroad organization.

During the World War II invasion of Normandy, Burpee landed with his Second Military Railway Service and thrust westward into the European continent. Colonel Burpee became commanding officer in the 703rd Railway Grand Division of the Allies during World War II a post that he held from 1941-1945. In this position, he was responsible for the entire railroad infrastructure in the European Theater of Operations.

To highlight the impressive work that Colonel Burpee and the Second Military Railway Service did, the following *Stars and Stripes* news article appeared in 1945.

> *All Aboard for Berlin,* NOTHING DAUNTS THE RAILROADERS
>
> THE Folligny yards in Normandy were covered by burned and twisted steel, charred railway cars, and rubble from blasted buildings. Bomb craters overlapped. The couple of skeleton buildings still standing became headquarters of the railroad battalion assigned to operate the line from Folligny to Le Mans . . .
>
> Running the military railroads on the continent is the job of the Second Military Railway Service, commanded by Brig. Gen. Clarence L. Burpee, of Jacksonville, Fla., who came into the service from the Atlantic Coast Lines. The majority of his officers and men are also former railroadmen, and their railway outfits now operating in France and Belgium originally were sponsored by railroads back home. The ace alumni of 35 U.S. lines are currently represented in every aspect of Army railroading on the continent.
>
> Military railways resemble civilian roads in organization. Headquarters of the Military Railways Service corresponds to the office of the general manager. Next comes grand

divisions, each of which is similar to the office of a general superintendent and operates a section of line. Under the grand divisions are the operating battalions to run the trains, and the shop battalions for heavy maintenance.

Since D-Day, the 2nd MRS has done a whopping job of hauling supplies to the front by virtue of its extraordinary organization and administration set-up. General Burpee's outfit inherited a railway system at a standstill. What our bombers hadn't smashed, the Germans had wrecked before they fled. The first job was to repair track, yards, telephone lines.

Most of the repairs of railway lines were handled by the Corps of Engineers. Since D-Day, their general service regiments repaired over 1500 miles of track, erected 100 railway bridges, rebuilt signal houses, marshalling yards, railway stations. One bridge thrown up by the engineers originally had been destroyed by American bombers, rebuilt by the Germans, smashed again by the R.A.F., and when finally captured was rebuilt once again by the engineers.

An interesting excerpt from a military paper of the war dubbed an express train for the furlough of military personnel as *Burpee's Bullet* for the expediency of getting soldiers on R/R from Bad-Godesberg, Germany to Namur, Belgium.

In May 1947, President Truman recommended to the United States Senate the appointment of Clarence Burpee to become a general officer. At approximately the same time, General Burpee was awarded the Distinguished Service Award and the Legion of Merit Award. On December 28, 1949, General Burpee was a passenger sailing on the *General Daniel I Sultan* from Yokohama, Japan to San Francisco, California.

As a tribute to General Burpee's long standing military career and his accomplishments during World War II, a United States Army Reserve Center located in Jacksonville, Florida was dedicated to him in 1957.

References:

California Passenger and Crew Lists, 1893-1957

Certified Death Certificate, Jacksonville, Florida

The New Georgia Encylopedia, 2008

Portland Press Herald, May 24, 1947, Page 9.

Portland Press Herald, November 30, 1947

Burpee Family, FTW, Internet Webpage

Destination—Berlin!, Stars & Stripes, Paris,1944-1945

The Yankee Bomber, Special Trains Carry GI's On Furlough, Volume 2, No. 44, August 2, 1945

USA Federal Census, 1900, 1910, 1920, 1930

WWI Draft Registration Card

Florida State Census, 1867-1945

Florida Death Index, Internet Webpage

Metro Jacksonville, Lost Jacksonville: Union Terminal, January 8, 2010

CLAUDE MCKINLEY BURPEE

Born: October 4, 1896, Athens, Clarke, Georgia, USA
Died: December 2, 1944, Augusta, Clarke, Georgia, USA
Buried: After December 2, 1944, Westover Memorial Park Cemetery, Lot
    3B, Augusta, Richmond, Georgia, USA

Occupation: Medical Doctor, Pediatric Specialty

Notable Accomplishment: Chief, Department of Pediatrics, University
    Hospital, Augusta, Georgia, USA

Claude McKinley Burpee was the second of nine children to Robert Alonzo Burpee and Lou Ellen Pitts. Claude grew up in Athens, Georgia. He registered for World War I on September 12, 1918. In 1920, Mr. Burpee received his undergraduate degree from the University of Georgia in Medicine. Two years later, Dr. Burpee graduated with his medical degree from the School of Medicine, University of Georgia.

After several years of residency at the University Hospital in Augusta, Georgia and post-graduate work at John Hopkins University Hospital, Baltimore, Maryland and Children's Hospital, Saint Louis, Missouri. Upon completing his training, Dr. Burpee returned to the University Hospital at Augusta where he assumed the position of Chief, Department of Pediatrics and held the title of Professor of Pediatrics.

On September 22, 1928, Claude married Margaret Lucille McLeod in Jefferson, Missouri. They had four children from this marriage.

References:

Georgia Alumni Record, December 1935, Page 83.
Burpee FTW, Internet Webpage
Missouri Marriage Records, 1805-2002
Georgia Death Records, 1919-1998
World War I Registration Card

DAVID BURPEE

Born: April 5, 1893, Philadelphia, Pennsylvania, USA
Died: June 24, 1980, Doylestown, Bucks, Pennsylvania, USA
Buried: After June 24, 1980, Doylestown Cemetery, 215 East Court
    Street, Doylestown, Bucks, Pennsylvania, USA

Occupation: President, W. Atlee Burpee and Company

Notable Accomplishment: America's largest mail order seed house

David Burpee was the oldest of three children born to Washington Atlee Burpee and Blanche Simmons. Mr. Burpee married Lois Torrance on July 18, 1938 in Norwalk, Fairfield, Connecticut, USA. David and Lois Burpee had two children, Jonathan and Blanche Elizabeth.

The following is a recounting of David's work in the company that bore his name:

David's father died in 1915, by which time his company was sending out a million catalogs a year. David, age 22 at the time, had to drop out of his college studies at Cornell University to became head of the firm. Soon after David Burpee took over the company's management, World War I precipitated a shortage of seeds—but also made America rather than Europe the world's leading seed supplier. Today, most Americans know about the reference to the Victory Gardens of World War II, but the "War Gardens" of World War I are all but forgotten.

Food will win the war, we were told by Washington and I decided the best way I could help our country's war effort was by showing people how to grow a good share of their food right in their own back yards. To dramatize this, I set up what we called War Gardens in a number of cities. The biggest attention-getter was the one in New York. It was in Union Square, directly opposite an imitation battleship bristling with wooden guns aimed at the tomatoes and cabbages. It was a huge success. I would guess that that garden alone must have started thousands of people gardening.

David Burpee had always been very close to his celebrated father and shared the same enthusiasms. From early childhood, the boy had been intrigued by the mysteries of plant genetics and had displayed a strong aptitude for creative gardening.

Only three years later after the death of his father, David found himself heading the firm at a critical time when war in Europe had begun to affect seed development and production in disastrous ways. Fortunately, he had the managerial assistance of his brother W. Atlee, Jr. and several very able executives and horticulturists, working as a team to overcome unexpected obstacles and maintain the momentum that had been built up by the founder.

A farming and gardening crisis arose in America when sources of seed withered as quickly as if countless plants had been killed by a devastating blight. Germany at that time was the world center of plant research and seed production, and other European nations-—France, Holland, and England in particular—also supplied a large percentage of seeds that were made suitable to American soil and climate through selective breeding at experimental facilities such as Burpee's Fordhook Farms near Doylestown, Pennsylvania.

Animosities between Germany and other European nations had been heating up for several years, and leaders in several American industries—including agriculture and horticulture-had long before foreseen both the possibility of a large scale war and the resulting disruptions in international trade. This was one of the reasons why W. Atlee Burpee had established Floradale Farms at Lompoc, California, in 1909. During World War I, his son David opened half a dozen regional breeding sites and sales offices in the USA and Mexico.

Throughout the war and afterward, both Fordhook and Floradale continued to develop extremely successful American flower and vegetable varieties from ancestral European stock. And in ensuing years, additional experimental/developmental stations would be opened in California, several other states, and even abroad.

Horticulture was David Burpee's driving passion, but by no means his sole interest. Although his father was his hero—the man he wished to emulate throughout his life—he keenly admired certain key characteristics of two more famous men.

One of these was Phineas T. Barnum, the celebrated showman who had all but invented the technique of the publicity campaign. This may puzzle horticultural historians for two reasons: David Burpee was a rather shy, unassuming person, whereas P.T. Barnum was a flamboyant extrovert; and whereas Barnum relished a good hoax, Burpee was notorious for his scrupulous honesty. In the latter respect, David invariably followed the example of his father, who had printed an apology to his customers in his 1914 catalog because he thought the cover picture showed a tomato larger than any that an average gardener could expect to grow. (A great many customers surprised him that year by sending him snapshots of giant tomatoes grown from his seeds—tomatoes rivaling the one on the cover!)

However, David Burpee, while insistent on total integrity, was quick to adopt and modernize the novel approach to promotion and advertising pioneered by Barnum. on one occasion, he had promotional leaflets dropped from an airplane—and Burpee was the world's first company to deliver seeds to customers by air. In 1911, W. Atlee first had seeds delivered by air when an important order missed a ship's sailing time. Unfortunately, when the package was dropped from the plane, it missed the boat and the seeds fell into the sea.

On another occasion, when he was about to introduce his first-of-their-kind Double Hybrid Nasturtiums in 1934, someone stole an enormous quantity of the seeds from an experimental field—a $25,000 loss that was especially shocking because industrial spying and theft are extremely rare in the horticultural business. Promotionally, at least, Burpee gleaned a profit from the loss by making sure the press thoroughly covered his hiring of a detective (who failed to track down the culprit) as well as his hiring of two armed deputy sheriffs to guard his next seed crop.

In subsequent decades, he "handed out seed packets the way John D. Rockefeller handed out dimes," to quote one reporter, and found numerous other ways to capture the nation's attention. He named flowers after Helen Hayes, Mamie Eisenhower, and Pennsylvania neighbor Pearl S. Buck, and he "starred" in one of Edward R. Murrow's "Person to Person" TV programs at his Pennsylvania headquarters (making sure the TV cameras captured his latest plant introductions). During World War II, Burpee vigorously promoted victory gardens, and although genuine patriotism was his primary motivation, the victory-garden movement was instrumental in turning non-farming Americans into vegetable gardeners, with Burpee as their foremost seed supplier. He desperately wanted to endow the 1945 catalog cover with a V-for-Victory (and victory-garden) theme, but the government would have frowned on the printing of a large symbolic V for commercial purposes. His art staff solved the problem very cleverly. The 1945 cover dominantly featured his new red chard, called Rhubarb Chard, in its natural shape—a great V. To the left of the V was his new orange-colored Jubilee Tomato, which at least some viewers have interpreted as symbolizing the globe. Above the V was a cluster of large, plump carrots—sufficiently bomb-shaped to help support the subliminal message.

Throughout David Burpee's career, he put great effort into the development of flowers and vegetables of many kinds, but new and improved marigolds were his greatest love, and by 1960 he had helped make marigolds America's most popular flower. That year, he registered as a lobbyist in Washington, D.C., and launched a campaign to have the marigold officially named the national flower. He enlisted the support of Senator Everett Dirksen of Illinois, who was eloquent in his championing of the marigold, telling the Senate, "Its robustness reflects the hardihood and character of the generations who pioneered and built this land into a great nation". For many years thereafter, Burpee made certain Dirksen was well supplied with marigolds every season. And Burpee himself engaged in well-publicized debates with Pennsylvania Senator Hugh Scott, who championed the rose. Most of the public also favored the rose, but all that opposition just served to provide unparalleled publicity for Burpee marigolds.

Indeed, marigolds were the focus of David Burpee's longest experimental project and greatest promotional exploit. In 1954, he offered a $10,000 prize to the first gardener who could provide seeds for a white marigold—something that simply didn't seem to exist. A pale lemon color was the closest his professional breeders had come. During the next two decades, more than 80,000 customers sent in seeds for testing. Some of them won $100 prizes for good tries, but the winner would have to produce a flower 2 1/2 inches wide and as white as Burpee's "Snowstorm" Petunia.

By 1975, Burpee's breeders had come closer than any of the submissions received with a variety called the "Snowbird", the whitest marigold developed to that day. At that point, Burpee and a panel of six horticultural professors reviewed the six top submissions and awarded the $10,000 to Alice Vonk, the widow of an Iowa farmer. Taking into account the contest costs, the prizes, and the development of the "Snowbird", that marigold was the world's costliest flower, but David Burpee considered the money well spent. Never had so many gardens across America been planted with marigolds

Just as Barnum inspired Burpee's quest for effective promotion, Napoleon—one of David's boyhood heroes—inspired certain aspects of his approach to business as well as plant development.

When Napoleon arranged for a shipment of Italian art treasures to France as war reparations, he intentionally invented many delays, and on the occasion of each delay, he sent off dispatches and letters to hone interest and arouse impatience among the art lovers of Paris. He was "teasing" his public, so to speak, and Burpee decided to adopt this tactic in publicizing and staging flower shows. Starting well in advance, Burpee would let the public know he had some new and splendid novelty to display, but he would keep it somewhat mysterious. When the show opened he would tell the story of the novelty's creation, keeping the novelty itself hidden from the audience until he had whipped up excited curiosity, and only then would he flick the curtain aside. "Napoleon," he said, "taught Maine how to give a flower show".

He also admired Napoleon's frequent military strategy of using speed and mobility—getting there first with the most and best-to achieve victory.

In 1933, when he was working almost feverishly to introduce the world's first double nasturtiums in a full range of colors, Burpee came down with typhoid fever and the project was delayed. Soon afterward, a couple of additional developmental setbacks made it seem that other seed men would win the race to unveil such hybrid nasturtiums.

Taking another lesson from Napoleon, Burpee reduced the project's schedule from three years to one, hired 200 extra workers to cross-pollinate flowers for a month in order to produce some 50,000 crosses, had the resulting seeds rushed from California to Pennsylvania by air mail, and by the following spring achieved another first.

Like Bonaparte, David Burpee was the kind of "general" who preferred to be with his troops—a very able immediate staff of management executives, sales people, logistics managers, and breeders. He was a peripatetic leader, always seeming to be on his way to or from somewhere (often accompanied by key staff members) to see growers, customers, horticultural experts, or anyone with a legitimate contribution to make to the improvement of flowers and vegetables. He took a direct hand in purchasing, production, and the development of new offerings. He became a leading expert in hybridization, his cherished specialty, and his Napoleonic campaigns in this specialty became his greatest contribution to American plant development and his greatest legacy for today's gardeners.

David Burpee was the first commercial horticulturist to recognize the potential of hybrids. His firm was to home gardening what Macintosh was to the development of personal computers. He believed-and proved-that he and his colleagues could revolutionize flower and vegetable growing, and at the same time make life easier and more enjoyable for gardeners. For example, a hybrid may require less fertilizer and less ideal soil than the parent strains, and less care throughout the growing season. Denis Flaschenriem, who was research manager at Burpee, once remarked that "we work for the modern-day gardener who doesn't want to do extra work like pinching off dead flowers to get the live ones to last." That objective isn't new; it was originated by D. B., as the staff called their leader.

In 1970, David Burpee sold his company to General Foods. In 1979 the company passed to ITT. David Burpee remained as a consultant until his death in June of 1980. In 1991 the Burpee Company was acquired by George J. Ball, Inc., a diversified horticultural family business. Jonathan Burpee, the founder's grandson, was the last family member to work for the company. He was fired by Ball in 1993.

References:

History Of The Burpee Seed Company, Internet Webpage
Seedsmen Hall of Fame, Seedsmen.org, Internet Webpage
Wikipedia, Internet Webpage

DAVID BURPEE

Born: April 22, 1752, Rowley, Essex, Massachusetts
Died: May 31, 1845, Maugerville, Sunbury, New Brunswick, Canada
Buried: After May 31, 1845, Sheffield United Church Cemetery, Sheffield,
   Sunbury, York, New Brunswick, Canada

Occupation: Farmer

Notable Accomplishments: Immigrant and Early Settler to Maugerville,
   New Brunswick, Canada; Magistrate and Office Holder

David Burpee was the eldest son of Jeremiah Burpee and Mary Saunders.
He was the eldest of eight children. David Married Elizabeth Gallishan on
January 1, 1778 in Maugerville, Sunbury, York, New Brunswick, Canada.
David and Elizabeth had fourteen of their own children (seven sons and
seven daughters).

It is believed that David received his formal education in Massachusetts
prior to moving to Canada. David immigrated with his parents between
1763 and 1764. His younger brother, Edward, was an American
sympathizer during the Revolutionary War and served in the Volunteer
Army to aid in the cause of the revolutionists.

David's father and grandfather assisted in founding the settlement of
Maugerville in what was then the colony of Nova Scotia. In its earliest
years, Maugerville operated as a traditional New England community,
with civil authority vested in town meetings and the church responsible
for social discipline.

The following description of David's life in Maugerville is excerpted from
several original documents of the day and edited by various researchers
over time:

> At age 19, after the death of his parents, David became
> responsible for his seven surviving brothers and sisters. Active,
> reticent, cautious, and systematic, he already showed the
> characteristics of his mature years. While pursuing his farm

chores, he had trained himself by keeping a diary, which is literate and meticulous, but silent regarding his personal views and ambitions. An account-book that notes each item he purchased or sold from 1772 to 1784 is an important source for historians in showing how values of goods and services fluctuated during the years of the American Revolution in a community where money was scarce and barter common. Historians owe him a further debt for his careful listing of the possessions left by his grandfather in 1781; it provides a rare insight into the style of living of a comparatively well-to-do frontier farmer.

The Burpee family shared the anti-British sentiments of their former compatriots in Massachusetts and David may have played some role in organizing Maugerville's support of the new Massachusetts government in 1775. Edward Burpee, a younger brother, joined Jonathan Eddy's expedition against Fort Cumberland (near Sackville, New Brunswick) the following year. In 1777 a British garrison was placed in Fort Howe (Saint John County) and six years later many Maugerville farms were taken over by American loyalists. Few of the newcomers had cause to respect the feelings of "rebels," and the old families, in turn, resented the favours granted to the intruders. Disturbed by the changes in their society and inspired by the New Light Ideas of Henry Alline, who had held "reformation" services in Maugerville in 1779 and 1781, some of the old inhabitants set themselves apart by withdrawing into a sectarian world of religious fervour. Among them were the followers of Archelaus Hammond, who advocated an antinomianism that led to bizarre forms of worship.

Although Burpee, who accepted the conservative Old Light Ideas of his grandfather Jonathan, was not prepared to compromise with the New Lights on theological matters, he nevertheless played a role in countering the deep divisions in his society and emerged as a moderating influence between the loyalist newcomers and the old inhabitants. In 1787 he and

Jacob Barker, Jr. received appointments as justices of the peace for Sunbury County, of which the township of Maugerville, now divided into the parishes of Maugerville and Sheffield, formed a part. These were positions of privilege, for authority no longer rested with town meetings, as in New England, but was vested in the justices, who met in the Court of General Sessions to administer county affairs.

The division of Maugerville township that had taken place in 1786 was reinforced by denominational differences. In the parish of Maugerville loyalist Anglicans were in the majority; in Sheffield old inhabitants predominated. When the Church of England in Maugerville claimed the public lot on which the old New England meeting-house stood, Burpee and Barker took the lead in 1789 in moving the building several miles downriver to a public lot in Sheffield, using 60 teams of oxen to haul it on the ice. That year the members of the Congregational Church signed a new covenant. All came from a small number of New England families, but their church was supported by immigrant Scots and other dissenters, including a few loyalists. For reasons which are unknown, though it seems probable that he considered himself unworthy, Burpee did not become a church member in terms of Congregational polity until 1805, yet he acted as clerk and served on all important committees. The congregation invited John James, a Calvinist Methodist from England, to be their pastor.

The appointment of this minister ended disastrously. In 1792, after being accused of drunkenness, association with persons of questionable character, and finally "scandalous indecencies" in his behaviour toward a young woman, James embraced the Church of England. The dissenters were able to regain possession of the parsonage, and the meeting-house of which it formed a part, only on 6 Aug. 1793 when, finding the premises temporarily vacated, Burpee entered and defied the authorities to expel him. By then the rupture between Anglicans and dissenters had become unbridgeable and dissenter abhorrence of Anglican exclusivism made Sunbury

County the centre of opposition to the policies of Lieutenant Governor Thomas Carleton. It was perhaps at this time that Burpee began a mutually helpful association with Samuel Denny Street, next to James Glenie, the leading opponent of the administration.

For the three decades ending in 1830 Burpee was one of his county's most active magistrates. He became a justice of the Inferior Court of Common Pleas and carried out a great deal of routine work, examining witnesses, signing recognizances, and binding persons to keep the peace. In 1814 he was appointed a justice of the quorum and made use of his office to get around the provision in the marriage law that required dissenters to be married by Anglican clergymen. Between January 1815 and September 1835 he performed 124 civil ceremonies in Sheffield. He also served as county auditor.

Burpee's participation in public affairs had behind it a firm commitment to the religious and social values of 17th-century New England Puritanism. While still comparatively young he became "Squire" Burpee, a patriarchal figure bent on restoring the fortunes of the dissenters' church and upholding Calvinist theology and traditional forms of worship in the face of New Light, Methodist, and Baptist appeals. His efforts reached fruition in 1820: the Sheffield congregation, reorganized and, for the time being, in communion with the Church of Scotland, was given title to a small portion of the land set aside for the church when the township of Maugerville was founded and finally obtained from Scotland a long-term resident pastor. Later, it reverted to its Congregational identity until it entered the United Church of Canada in 1925.

When Burpee's son David died in 1830, he received a long obituary in provincial papers. Although he was county treasurer and church deacon, the notice was really a recognition of his father, then in his 78th year and still an active magistrate. Among the documents old David left when he died at the age of 93 is one entitled "Record Book kept by the Town

Clerk of Sheffield Sunbury County 1767-1835." It is a fitting memorial to his career, for he had preserved the spirit of the old Maugerville township, and by continuing its records had made it possible for the story of the persistence of a frontier community to be known to later generations

References:

Burpee FTW, Internet Webpage

Lineage and Decendents of Jeremiah Burpee, Webpage, ngraves4.tribalpages.com

Marriages Found In the Chruch Records Of Sheffield For Settlers Of Maugerville,

Record Book kept by the Town Clerk of Sheffield Sunbury County 1767-1835 by David Burpee, New Brunswick Museum, Sheffield, New Brunswick, Canada, edited by William McLeod, typescript 1937

Maugerville School, 1763-1951 by F. M. Miles, typescript, 1951.

Documents of the Congregational Church at Maugerville, New Brunswick Historic Society, Coll., 1 (1894-97), no1: 119-52; no.2: Pages 153-159.

Documents relating to Sunbury County: David Burpee's diary, New Brunswick Historic Society., Coll., 1, no.l: Pages 89-95.

The Newlight Baptist Journals of James Manning and James Innis, ed. D. G. Bell, Saint John County, New Brunswick, Canada, 1984

The Pickard Papers, ed. Gerald Keith, New Brunswick Historic Society., Coll., no.15 (1959): Pages 55-78.

Sunbury County Documents, New Brunswick Historic Society, Coll., 1, no.1: Pages 100-118.

Head Quarters, or Literary, Political, and Commercial Journal (Fredericton), 4 June 1845

DAVID BURPEE, III

Born: April 12 1827, Sheffield, Sunbury, York, New Brunswick, Canada
Died: September 14 1882, Philadelphia, Pennsylvania, USA
Buried: September 18, 1882, Woodlands Cemetery, Section H, Lots 6-7,
    4000 Woodland Avenue, Philadelphia, Pennsylvania, USA

Occupation: Prominent Medical Doctor and Surgeon

David Burpee, III was the youngest of seven children of David Burpee, II and Sarah E. Coburn. David married Ann Catherine (Kate) Atlee on June 5, 1855 in Philadelphia, Pennsylvania. David and Ann Catherine had three children. Of note, was their eldest son Washington Atlee Burpee. W. Atlee Burpee was the founder of the Burpee Seed Company of Philadelphia, Pennsylvania. Ann Catherine's father, Dr. Washington Lemuel Atlee, was a nationally known obstetric surgeon of the time who specialized in the removal of ovarian cancers.

David Burpee, III attended the Sheffield Grammar School in Sheffield, New Brunswick, Canada. Mr. Burpee went on to study the Classics at Mount Allison, Wesleyan Academy from 1845-1847. His first cousin, Dr. Humphrey Pickard, was the principal of this institution at the time.

Mr. Burpee went on to be a very successful practicing physician in the Philadelphia area. Often, he worked with Dr. Washington Atlee on medical cases.

References:

Burpee FTW, Internet Webpage

Email from Rhianna Edwards, University Archivist, Mount Allison University, Sackville, New Brunswick, Canada, February 10, 2009

A Genealogical Study by Winthrop Pickard Bell, published 1962

Wesleyan Academy Calendars, 1845-1848

The American Journal Of The Medical Sciences, Article X—Cases of Ovariotomy, July 1872

EDGAR ALPHONSO BURPEE

Born: December 19, 1839, Rockland, Knox, Maine, USA
Died: January 11, 1919, Rockland, Knox, Maine, USA
Buried: January 11, 1919, Achorn Cemetery, Rockland, Knox, Maine, USA

Occupation: Business Owner, Funeral Home

Notable Accomplishment: Captain, Civil War, Union, 19th Regiment, Company 1, Maine Volunterrs

Edgar Burpee was the eldest of five children born to Nathaniel Adams Burpee and Mary Jane Partridge. His father, Nathaniel, was a noted business man in the Rockland area. In addition to his father's notoriety, William Partridge Burpee, a sibling of Edgar's was a famous painter. Both of these individuals will be covered later in this biographic collection.

Edgar Alphonso Burpee married Annie Eliza Farwell on November 20, 1866 in Rockland, Knox, Maine. Edgar and Annie had two children during their marriage. They were Frances Farwell and Ada Carleton.
Edgar Burpee is remembered for his participation in the Civil War. He enlisted in the Union Army on August 25, 1862. More precisely, he is remembered for his written reflections, as an officer in the Maine, Nineteenth Infantry Regiment, Company I. In addition to these writings, Captain Burpee spent nine months as a prisoner of war before being exchanged in a soldier swap and discharged from the Union Army on May 15, 1864.

In July of 1863, the 19th Maine participated in the Gettysburg Campaign under Major General Winfield Scott Hancock, commander of the II Corps. On the third day of fighting (July 3) the 19th Maine was on top of Cemetery Ridge and faced Pickett's Charge.

On July 22, 1863 Edgar wrote to his mother about his emotions while facing a heavy artillery bombardment and then the famous Pickett's Charge.

> "It was a trying moment when with a single line we rose up to breast the storm of lead from the enemies guns. The men dropped so fast that it seemed for a moment as if we should be overpowered and slain but the thought of retreating never occurred to Maine. And when we charged down the hill the enemy fleeing in confusion, though shell and grape was coming like a hurricane, the only thoughts I had were to press forward."

This letter goes on to describe the feeling of shot, shell, noise, and confusion felt by the Union troops on Cemetery Ridge.

> "Then mother you cannot conceive the terrible shriek and noise of shell and appalling report grape and cannister make when it strikes the ground. It almost makes a man shudder & cringe to be a listener to it. It requires much strength of mind to compose oneself when lying under a rapid shelling, but strange as it may seem one can get accustomed to it and even sleep while it is going on."

In a separate letter to his sister shortly after the Battle of Gettysyburg, Captain Burpee expresses a piece of war humor. The Confederate Color Bearer,

> "kept dipping his 'infernal rag' at us" and "we gave the rebs a few pills that made their heads and stomachs ache" and "could I have got a hold of that fellow who carried the flag I would have knocked his head off."

And a piece of written battle grief for a fallen soldier,

> "I could hardly keep from crying . . . our much loved Capt. Smith was dying . . . how much I miss him. All along our march I am reminded of him. All he has ever said to me keeps coming to my mind. I cannot realize he has gone forever. All this spring he has kept telling about going home in September on a furlough and what he was going to do and when we arrived next to Gettysburg he said he hoped we were going into a fight so he could say he had done something for his country. I have his account book and his blood is on some of its leaves. Every time I look at it I almost shudder to think it was the life blood of my dear friend."

These excerpts are but a small sample of writings by a combat officer who provided leadership at this most famous battle.

Ironically, he returned to Rockland, Maine and in 1872 joined his father and uncle in their established funeral business that still carries their family name to this day. Edgar continued operating the funeral business until the family sold it to R. M. Leach on May 25, 1919

References:

Burpee Family FTW, Internet Webpage

Edgar Burpee Papers, 1863, Pearce Civil War Collection, Navarro College, Corsicana, Texas

The History of Thomaston, Rockland and South Thomaston, Maine Volume 2, Page 60.

Ebenezer Burpee's Last Will and Testament

USA Federal Census, 1850, 1870, 1900, 1910

Union Officer Prisoners Imprisoned Prison(s), Internet Webpage

Burpee, Carpenter and Hutchins Funeral Home, Internet Webpage.

ELLEN FRANCES BURPEE

Born: November 14, 1840, New Hampton, Belknap, New Hampshire, USA

Died: January 6, 1907, Naples, Napoli, Campania, Italy

Buried: After January 6, 1907, Glenwood Cemetery, Littleton, Grafton, New Hampshire, USA

Occupation: Painter, Floral, Still Lifes, and Southwesten Style Mission

Notable Accomplishments: Exhibitions in 1890 to 1892, California State Fair; 1893 Worlds Columbian Expo in Chicago

Ellen Frances Burpee was the eldest of the four children of Augustus Burpee and Sarah Glines Robinson. Ellen was a graduate of the New Hampton Institute and Thetford Academy. She married Civil War hero and United States Congressman Everts Worcester Farr on May 19, 1861 in Portsmouth, Rockingham, New Hampshire, USA. Ellen and Everts moved to his hometown of Littleton, New Hampshire. They had three children: Ida Louise, Herbert Augustus and Edith May.

Her paintings captured various missions, pepper trees and still lifes of Native American baskets, fish, game, and floral. These paintings found ready markets throughout the United States.

After the death of her husband in 1880, she moved to Boston for several years. In 1887, she went to California and began the most productive period of her career. In Pasadena, she bought an old vineyard and built a mission style studio on the property. She became one of Pasadena's most prominent artists. Her artwork was exhibited at the California State Fair from 1890 to 1892 and at the Worlds Columbian Expo in Chicago in 1893.

In December of 1906, she moved to Naples, Italy for her health and to enjoy the European masterpieces. She passed away approximately five weeks after moving to Italy. Due to the superstitious nature of crew members of a cargo ship that was to take her remains back to the United States, she was clandestinely stowed in a crate and labeled as a sculpture Today, her art work is on permanent display at the Littleton Public Library, Littleton, New Hampshire and the Washington County Historical Society, Washington, Pennsylvania.

References:

An Encyclopedia of Women Artists of the American West by Phil Kovinick and Marian Yoshiki-Kovinick
Personal Account of Ellen Farr by Sandy Coflan Martin, a direct descendent
Artists in California, 1786-1940 by Edan Hughes
USA Federal Census, 1850, 1860 and 1880
Burpee Family FTW, Internet, Webpage
Artists of the American West by Doris Dawdy
Southern California Artists by Nancy Moure
Women Artists of the American West
Pasadena Daily News, Obituary, January 8, 1907

FRANK EUGENE BURPEE

Born: May 16, 1872, Beloit, Mitchell, Kansas, USA
Died: November 29, 1958, Lewisburg, Union, Pennsylvania, USA
Burial: After November 29, 1958, Unknown Location

Occupation: College Professor

Notable Accomplishment: Created the Mechanical Engineering
Department at Bucknell University, Pennsylvania

Frank Eugene Burpee was one of five children of Nathan Louis Burpee
and Mary Suzanne Gifford. His family later moved to Pennsylvania. He
received a Bachelor of Arts degree from Bucknell University in 1901 and
a Master of Arts degree in 1902.

After graduation, he was Professor of Greek and Assistant in Mathematics
at Leland University, New Orleans, Louisiana. He returned to Lewisburg
and served as Instructor in Greek and Latin in the Academy from 1902 to
1905. In 1905 he was appointed as an Instructor in Mathematics in the
College, at a salary of $1,200.00 per annum. At the same time he was also
appointed superintendent of buildings and grounds, with control of all
persons employed in the care of the buildings, including the heating and
lighting plant.

He married Pearl Lois Smith in 1905. They had two children: Evelyn Mae and Stanley Franklin.

In 1908, he became Assistant Professor of Mathematics and Superintendent of Buildings and Grounds at Bucknell University. He did graduate work at the University of Michigan from 1906 to 1908 and at the University of Chicago in 1909.

Bucknell University President John Howard Harris selected him to develop a department of mechanical engineering and in 1913 he was appointed Professor of Mechanical Engineering. In 1931, John B. Stetson University awarded Professor Burpee an honorary Doctor of Engineering degree. Until 1936, Professor Burpee served as a professor at Bucknell University carrying a full load of teaching, and in addition the work of Superintendent of Buildings and Grounds. He retired from teaching in 1937 but continued to serve as Superintendent of Buildings and Grounds until his final retirement in 1944.

He was involved in many building projects on the campus. He supervised the building of Carnegie Library, Harris Hall, East College, the Foundry, the First Wing of the Engineering Building, Hunt Hall, the Women's Dining Hall, and the Botany Building. He was also a consulting engineer for the construction of Memorial Stadium.

Frank Eugene Burpee was very active in community affairs. He was a member of the Lewisburg Borough Council for many years and served as its president. He also served as the Burgess of Lewisburg. He was a member of the William Cameron Engine Company and the Lewisburg Baptist Church.

As an interesting footnote, David Burpee, President of W. Atlee Burpee Seed Company (also profiled in this book) endowed a chair at Bucknell University for the study of plant genetics. This chair is still ongoing

References:

Biography & Genealogy Master Index [database online]. Provo, Utah: MyFamily.com, Inc, 2005

USA Federal Census, 1900, 1910, 1930

New York Times, Obituary, November 30, 1958

World War One, Draft Registration Card

Institute for Broadening Participation, Internet Webpage, http://www.pathwaystoscience.org/programhub.asp?sort=PDC-Bucknell University-EndowedChair

FREDERICK TODD BURPEE, II

Born: February 14, 1917, Orono, Penobscot, Maine, USA
Died: April 9, 2007, Orono, Penobscot, Maine, USA
Buried: After April 9, 2007, Riverside Cemetery, Orono, Penobscot,
    Maine, USA

Occupation: House construction; Owner, F.T. Burpee Hardware

Notable Accomplishment: Captain, U.S. Army, Ambulance Corps, World
    War II, evacuated 14,000 wounded troops at Normandy and Battle
    of the Bulge

Frederick Todd Burpee, II was one of seven children born to Merritt
Lemuel Burpee and Mary Pearl Gothrow. He was named after his
grandfather. Both of his parents were born in New Brunswick, Canada
and immigrated to the State of Maine prior to 1907.

He graduated from Orono High School in 1934, and was a member of
the 1932 undefeated and unscored upon, Orono High School football
team. He graduated from Higgins Classical Institute and attended the
University of Maine. About 1943, Frederick married Ruth Arlene Virgie
in Orono, Maine. They had three children: Marilyn B, Bette Anne and
Frederick Todd III.

At the outbreak of World War II, he served as a captain in the U.S. Army with the 583rd Ambulance Company. Captain Burpee's company evacuated more than 14,000 wounded troops at Normandy and the Battle of the Bulge. He was also in the Ardennes, Northern France and Central Europe theaters, and was awarded the Purple Heart during the Battle of the Bulge. Fred's favorite vocation and avocation was carpentry.

At the conclusion of the war, he worked for many years with his father building homes in the Orono area. Fred is best known for his hometown store, F.T. Burpee Hardware, which he owned and operated for 14 years in Orono village. For 10 years, Fred worked for the Farmer's Home Administration as a building inspector and assistant county supervisor.

Retirement in 1979 gave Fred many more days at Pushaw Lake and the beloved cottage he built with his dad in 1936. He was very community minded serving in Kiwanis, was and the Jaycees. He was a member of the American Legion Post No. 84 in Orono and served on many town committees. Fred was a charter member of the Church of Universal Fellowship. Fred's involvement in the community and love of sports and especially of good sportsmanship, prompted him to establish the F.T. Burpee Good Sportsmanship Award in 1949. It continues to this day and is awarded annually to a deserving athlete in the junior class of Orono High School.

References:

Burpee Family FTW, Internet Webpage
Social Security Death Index
USA Federal Census, 1920, 1930
National Archives and Records Administration, US Army Enlistment Records

GEORGE EGERTON RYERSON BURPEE

Born: November 10, 1834, Sheffield, Sunbury, York, New Brunswick, Canada

Died: November 26, 1904, St. Margaret's Hospital, Boston, Middlesex, Massachusetts, USA

Buried: November 28, 1904, Mount Hope Cemetery, Plot 1272CG, Bangor, Maine, USA

Occupation: Engineer, Lumber Executive, Railroad Builder

Notable Accomplishment: Building several railroad lines between Northern Maine and Canada

Mr. Burpee was one of eight children of Isaac Burpee and Phoebe Elizabeth Coburn. Mr. Burpee's grandparents immigrated from Massachusetts and became among the earliest inhabitants of the Sheffield area. Like all of Isaac and Phoebe's children, George left the farm of his parents and became successful in business. George Egerton Ryerson Burpee married Louise Godfry Thissell in Bangor, Penobscot, Maine on January 20, 1870. They had one child who survived infancy. Louise Coburn Burpee was born on May 9, 1877 and married William Otis Sawtelle. Dr. Sawtelle was a noted physicist employed at the Massachusetts Institute of Technology.

Mr. Burpee was the brother-in-law of centenarian Senator David Wark of Fredericton, New Brunswick, Canada.

Mr. Burpee's biography is summarized in the following passage from a book reflecting notables of the time.

Mr. George Egerton Ryerson Burpee, a graduate of the University of New Brunswick, an engineer of recognized standing, and one of the most successful and largest operators in lumbering enterprises in Northern Maine, was a native of Canada, having been born at Sheffield, New Brunswick, in that country, in November, 1834. His death, which occurred on Thanksgiving Day, November 25, 1904, at St. Margaret's Hospital, Boston, Massachusetts, was felt as a severe loss by the city of Bangor, of which he was one of the most prominent and influential citizens.

Mr. Burpee, in the services which he rendered in connection with the upbuilding and development of this region, gave a fair exchange for the title of "American citizen," which he assumed upon coming to live in this region, and which he was always proud to bear, although his heart continued warm and true to his native Canadian province. He won much fame as an engineer and builder of railroads, and as one of those men who developed the lumber interests of Maine to its present great importance.

Mr. Burpee was also an Egyptologist of note, but for none of these things will he be remembered so long and with such affection as for his Christian philanthropy. He was a man of deep and true Christian character, and was always helpful to those about him, contributing constantly through many channels to the relief of suffering and distress. Large of body and mind, his heart was in proportion, and he was readily touched by human misfortune of any kind.

A member of the Central Congregational Church from the time of his corning to Bangor, it was largely through his devotion that the beautiful church edifice which stood on French street, and has since been burned, became a reality, he being the largest contributor towards its erection. Force of character, allied with brilliant talents, brought him an eminence in his profession in the East, and success in the business world he entered.

George Egerton Ryerson Burpee was a son of Isaac and Phoebe (Coburn) Burpee, the former a native of Massachusetts. Isaac Burpee was taken early in life to New Brunswick, Canada, by his parents, where he married, and where his six children were born. He passed the remainder of his life in New Brunswick, and both his death and that of his wife occurred in that country.

George Egerton Ryerson Burpee, or as he was always called, Egerton R Burpee, was given all the advantages of an education in good intermediate and preparatory schools, and later entered the University of New Brunswick, at Fredericton. He had already determined upon an engineering course, and after pursuing this line of study was graduated as a civil engineer. He at once plunged into active professional work and in a few years had attained a high reputation as an engineer and builder of railroads in the Dominion of Canada. His first important work was the construction of a railroad from St. Andrews to Quebec Junction, near Houlton, Maine, the planning and superintendence of its construction being his own work. His next notable achievement was the construction of the present line of railroad between St. Johns, New Brunswick, and Bangor, Maine.

As already stated, he was a large operator in lumber interests in the northern part of the State, and finally made his home at Bangor, where his death occurred. Mr. Burpee was a member of the Central Congregational Church of Bangor, which is now known as All Soul's Church, and was deeply interested in its welfare. During his entire life he was by nature a student, and became deeply interested in Egyptian history and the learning of the ancients. He and Mrs. Burpee visited Egypt on several occasions, and on one of these spent several months there, but during this time Mr. Burpee was unfortunately very ill and unable to do much in the way of exploration.

George Egerton Ryerson Burpee was united in marriage, in January, 1870, shortly after locating to Bangor, with Louise

Godfrey Thissell, daughter of James and Louise (Godfrey) Thissell, a descendant on both sides of the house from old and distinguished Maine families. Mr. and Mrs. Burpee were the parents of one daughter, Louise, who became the wife of Professor William Otis Sawtelle. Professor and Mrs. Sawtelle are the parents of five children, as follows: Egerton, Louise, Eleanor, Janet and Margery.

References:

A History of Maine, Biographical, Centennial Edition, The American Historical Society, New York, 1919, Pages 74-75.

Piety Portrayed In The Lives and Deaths of Mr. and Mrs. Isaac Burpee of Sheffield, New Brunswick by Robert Wilson, Wesleyan Minister, Printed by H. Chubb, 1870

Boston Globe, Obituary, November 1904

Burpee Family FTW, Internet Webpage

Census of Canada, 1861

Marriage Returns of Penobscot County, Maine, Volume 6, Page 502.

USA Federal Census, 1880

HARRY BALDWIN BURPEE

Born: July 11, 1861, Rockford, Winnebago, Illinois, USA
Died: April 06, 1947, Rockford, Winnebago, Illinois, USA
Burial: April 09, 1947, Greenwood Cemetery, Rockford, Winnebago, Illinois, USA

Occupation: Owner, Funeral Home

Notable Accomplishment: Established the Burpee Museum of Natural History

Harry Baldwin Burpee was one of five children born to Alpheus Crosby Burpee and Harriet Maria Baldwin. Harry married Della C. Trufant in October 11, 1883 in Rockford, Illinois. Upon her death, he married Myra Savage Cook December 27, 1937. All three are buried in Greenwood Cemetery, Rockford, Illinois.

Harry's father started a funeral home in 1856. Later, his father branched into the furniture industry that was a strong industry in Rockford. Harry worked in both the retail furniture business and as an undertaker in the funeral home.

Harry and his 1st wife, Della, are best remembered for opening the Harry and Della Burpee Art Museum in 1936. It later became the Rockford Art Museum. Della commissioned the sarcophagus where she and her husband were laid to rest in Greenwood Cemetery.

Currently, the Burpee Museum of Natural History is housed in two Victorian era mansions. At one time, one was owned by the Manny family famous for the Manny Reapers. The other belonged to the John Barnes family. This family was also important in developing Rockford into a manufacturing town. The other belonged to the John Barnes family. This family was also important in developing Rockford into a manufacturing town.

References:

Northwest Quarterly, Spring 2010, Pages 134-135.
Advertising Pamphlets for Burpee and Wood Funeral Home
USA Federal Census 1870, 1900, 1920, 1930
Find-A-Grave Internet, Website

ISAAC BURPEE, JR.

Born: November 23, 1825, Sheffield, Sunbury, York, New Brunswick, Canada

Died: March 02, 1885, New York, New York, USA

Buried: After March 02, 1885, Fernhill Cemetery, Westmoreland Road, Saint John, New Brunswick, Canada

Cause of Death: Bright's Disease

Occupation: Hardware Merchant; Partial owner of the New Brunswick Railroad

Notable Accomplishment: Member, Canadian Parliament, Saint John, New Brunswick area

Isaac Burpee was a merchant, entrepreneur, and politician from the New Brunswick Province. He was the eldest son of Isaac Burpee and Phoebe Elizabeth Coburn. He married Henrietta Robertson on March 8, 1855. Isaac, Jr. and Henrietta had eight children. Isaac's grandfather was one of the earliest settlers to immigrate from the Rowley, Massachusetts area to the Saint John River County area.

> Isaac Burpee, the descendant of pre-loyalist settlers, was educated at the Sheffield Grammar School and in 1848 moved to Saint John, New Brunswick. There, with his brother Frederick, he established a flourishing hardware business which by 1872 had become a "wholesale only" establishment selling not only small wares but also significant quantities of imported and domestic iron and steel. In the 1860s he

purchased valuable property in Saint John and a home in the suburb of Portland (now part of Saint John), and by 1872 the assessed value of his personal and real estate in the city was $70,000.

As Burpee's fortune grew, he began investing in a variety of industrial enterprises based on his hardware company in Saint John. In partnership with Howard Douglas Troop, he established in 1882 a steamship line between London, Halifax, and Saint John, but the endeavour failed when the sole boat operated by the partners was wrecked on its second voyage.

In 1883 Burpee and some associates purchased the Coldbrook Rolling Mills north of Saint John to produce iron and steel forms, nails, and spikes. His other interests were in the Confederation Life Association, the New Brunswick Land and Lumber Company, the Red Granite Company, which held property in Saint John and Charlotte counties, the Victoria Coal Mining Company, and the Saint John Cotton Company. Beginning in the early 1870s Burpee was heavily involved in the financing, construction, and operation of railways in the province. The Central Railway Company, with which his brother, Egerton Ryerson Burpee, and his uncle, Charles Burpee, were also involved, was to link Fredericton with Saint John, but construction was not begun until 1887. The New Brunswick Railway Company was to link Fredericton with Edmundston, via Woodstock, and opened for service in 1878. Burpee felt that not only would his hardware company and rolling-mills supply materials for the railways' construction, but that the lines would run through lumber and coal-bearing lands he owned throughout the province. However, Burpee's attempt to create an extended economic empire was not particularly successful; by 1884 he had made valuable investments but was struggling to show an operating profit on his holdings. Perhaps the demands of his wide-ranging business activities, coupled with an active career in federal politics, were too great for his energies and financial resources.

Burpee had first entered political life when he led the movement to incorporate Portland and became the first chairman of the town council in 1871. The following year he was elected member of parliament for the City and County of Saint John with an overwhelming majority. Originally an independent who supported Sir John A. Macdonald's government, Burpee became convinced over the summer and fall of 1873 of the government's culpability in the Pacific Scandal and on 31 October joined the ranks of the Liberal opposition. A week later he was sworn in as minister of customs in Alexander Mackenzie's cabinet, after Protestant members of parliament for New Brunswick, including three of Burpee's relatives, had pressured Mackenzie into appointing him rather than the Irish Catholic, Timothy Warren Anglin. As customs minister until 1878, Burpee appears to have been efficient, knowledgeable, and conscientious. Although he was easily re-elected in Saint John in 1874, 1878, and 1882, he was not a notably skilful politician; Mackenzie thought him "a model office man but not good for six sentences in the House and no parliamentary knowledge.

Burpee looked upon public service as an obligation to be fulfilled and concerned himself in politics mainly with business matters. His economic philosophy was typical of the 19th century laissez-faire school. He believed that individual enterprise and energy, not government legislation and protection, were the keys to personal and national progress. Like his colleagues in the Reform party in the 1870s, he accepted that depressions were natural, if unfortunate, and that the government's role was to pare expenditures, keep down the public debt, and maintain tariffs at the lowest possible levels. Burpee apparently had no doubts, therefore, about opposing the protectionist National Policy of the Macdonald Conservatives during and after the 1878 federal election. He argued that the protective tariff was unfair to consumers, especially the poor and labourers, that it aided the interests of on and Quebec at the expense of the Maritime provinces, that it was antithetical to the British connection, and that it would promote urbanization at the expense of rural, agricultural interests. Perhaps most important, he felt the high tariff favoured not the majority of manufacturers but only a specific few such as sugar refiners and cotton and woollen manufacturers. Burpee's efforts to promote industrial activity in New Brunswick in the 1880s may well have been, therefore, a defensive and unwilling response to the protective tariff, and his lack of any great success in his own endeavours probably confirmed his negative opinion of the National Policy.

Although his being an important businessman undoubtedly aided Burpee's political career, it also presented problems. In November 1873 a cry was raised about the propriety of selecting a large importer as minister of customs, and as a result Burpee retired, at least pro forma, from his hardware firm. This was but one of several conflict of interest accusations levelled at him while he was minister. Even after the defeat of the Liberals in 1878, Burpee was accused by newspapers opposed to him in the 1882 election of attempting to manipulate import duties imposed by Washington on incoming lumber in such a way as to injure the sawmilling industry of Saint John and increase traffic on the New Brunswick Railway, of which he was vice-president. The significance of business affairs in Burpee's political career can also be seen in the fact that James Domville, Conservative MP for Kings County from 1872 to 1882, was Burpee's most consistent political antagonist as well as a business competitor.

Besides his activities in business and politics, Burpee gave of his time and money to a number of charitable or social agencies, including the New Brunswick Deaf and Dumb Institute, the Saint John Industrial School, the Portland Free Public Library, the Saint Paul's Sunday School House, and the Marysville Methodist Church. He showed an interest in such community endeavours as the Saint John centennial celebrations in 1883 and the New Brunswick Historical Society, founded in 1874. He also held executive positions on the Congregational Union of New Brunswick and Nova Scotia and the Evangelical Alliance of New Brunswick during the 1870s.

The last two years of Burpee's life were unhappy. Aside from business problems, his second son was drowned in July 1883 and his younger brother was killed in a train accident the following year. These tragedies gave Burpee a feeling of impending doom. "The sad bereavements we have passed through," he wrote Edward Blake, "has made me feel as if something harder would soon come again. I have been tending more to my private affairs in consequence, and almost feel afraid to leave my family." His sense of foreboding proved correct for, after putting his affairs in order, he died of either liver or heart disease in New York City in March 1885.

Though not a politician of major significance, Burpee was a notable example of the involved 19th-century Canadian entrepreneur. As a hard-working, efficient, and upstanding businessman, he had managed to accumulate an estate valued at his death at approximately $200,000.

References:

Burpee FTW, Internet Webpage
Saint John County, Newspaper, Editorial, March 1885
New York Times, Obituary, March 1885

JAMES HENRY ABIEL BURPEE

Born: March 23, 1839, New London, Merrimack, New Hampshire, USA

Died: February 9, 1923, Medford, Middlesex, Massachusetts, USA

Burial: After February 9, 1923, Unknown location

Occupation: Businessman

Notable Accomplishments: Served on the staffs of several Governors of the State of New Hampshire; Assistant Secretary of State, New Hampshire, USA; College Trustee for Colby-Sawyer College, New London, New Hampshire

James Henry Abiel Burpee was the youngest of three children born to Abiel Burpee and Mary Messenger Woodbury. James married Stella Permelia Weston in Chester, Vermont on September 8, 1864. James and Stella had, in turn, three children of their own. James was a fourth generation Burpee living in New London, New Hampshire. His grandfather and great-grandfather, Asa Burpee and Thomas Burpee, respectively, migrated from Rowley, Massachusetts to New London, New Hampshire prior to 1790. This migration made the Burpee family one of the earliest settlers to the New London, New Hampshire area.

In August 27, 1862, James answered the call of duty for his Country. He enlisted in Company K, 9th Infantry Regiment, New Hampshire

Volunteers on August 29, 1862. Later, he was discharged for disability reasons from Company K, 9th Infantry Regiment New Hampshire on 25 February 1863 in Baltimore, Maryland.

Mr. Burpee served briefly as the Assistant Secretary of State for the State of New Hampshire.

In 1897, he served as a college trustee for Colby-Sawyer College, New London, Merrimack County, New Hampshire. His service to the college was one of many Burpee family members who gave of their time and resources during the early years of its establishment.

References:

Burpee Family FTW, Internet Webpage

Register of Soldiers and Sailors of New Hampshire 1861-65, Massachusetts GAR: Journal of the Annual Encampment GAR Dept of Massachusetts 1866-1947

USA Federal Census 1850, 1870, 1900, 1920

Revised Register of the Soldiers and Sailors of New Hampshire in the War of the Rebellion, 1861-1866, published 1895, Page 467.

The First Century of Colby by Henry K Rowe, 1937, Page 398.

Boston Globe, Obituary, February 1923

JAMES STANLEY BURPEE

Born: February 12, 1938 Alameda, Alameda, California, USA
Died: Not Applicable
Burial: Not Applicable

Occupation: Artist/Painter

Notable Accomplishment: Paintings in both private and corporate
   collections

James Stanley Burpee was the son of Stanley Preston Burpee and Ruth
Belle Fonda. James married Gloria Renee Morales on August 6, 1960 in
El Cerrito, Contra Costa, California. They had three children: Paul James,
Laura Maria and Maria Danielle.

The same year of their marriage, James graduated from California College
of Arts and Crafts with a Masters' in Fine Arts. From 1967 to 1996,
he taught at the Minneapolis College of Art College of Art & Design,
Minneapolis, Minnesota. Since 1997, he has been affiliated with the
University of Minnesota, Minneapolis, Minnesota as an Adjunct Professor
in the Faculty Painting & Drawing Department.

Later in his life, he was married two more times. Secondly, he married
Patricia Fonda. Lastly, he married Mary Manning. He is currently
divorced.

For the past four decades, James Burpee has frequently shown his paintings
at single, two person and group exhibitions throughout the State of
Minnesota. He has traveled and studied in his profession throughout

Italy, France and England. Most recently, James has published a book on his art work entitled, *James Burpee; paintings & drawings 1960-2004*. His paintings are in private and corporate collections throughout Minnesota, New York and Hawaii.

Since 2000 he had made a commitment to paint from nature. The paintings are from creeks on the North Shore of Lake Superior in Minnesota that have an incredible richness of form and color. The play of light, the flow of water, and the sculptural boulders and rocks are the main subjects. The viewpoint is intimate rather than picturesque of scenic. His primary process is to convert photographs of nature into paintings.

References:

Personal email correspondence, 2010
James Burpee, Personal Website, WWW.jamesburpee.com
California Birth Index, 1905-1995
Minnesota Marriage Collection, 1958-2001

JOSEPH BURPEE

Born: September 25, 1765, Sheffield, Sunbury, York, New Brunswick, Canada

Died: October 10, 1830, Sheffield, Sunbury, York, New Brunswick, Canada

Buried: After October 10, 1830, Sheffield, Sunbury, York, New Brunswick, Canada

Occupation: Unknown

Notable Accomplishment: First Burpee born in Canada

Mr. Joseph Burpee was born to Jeremiah Burpee and Mary Sanders on September 25, 1765 in Sheffield, New Brunswick, Canada. He was the youngest of eight children born to his parents. Of particular historical note, he is believed to be the first Burpee born in Canada after the migration of Burpee family members in 1764 (his father and grandfather and their immediate families) from Rowley, Massachusetts to Sheffield, New Brunswick, Canada area.

Joseph Burpee married Abigail Gallishan on December 1, 1789 Sheffield, Sunbury, York, New Brunswick, Canada. Together, they raised eleven children (six females and 5 males) that were all born and raised in Sheffield, New Brunswick, Canada. Little else is known about his life.

References:

Acadia French Catholic Church Records, Drouin Collection, 1670-1946
Ancestry.com Internet Database
Burpee Family Tree, FTW, Internet Webpage

LAWRENCE JOHNSTONE BURPEE

Born: 05 Mar 1873, Halifax, Nova Scotia, Canada
Died: October 13, 1946, Oxford, England
Buried: After October 13, 1946, Beechwood Cemetery, Ottawa, Ontario,
    Canada

Occupation: Historian, a civil servant, a librarian and a writer

Notable Accomplishments: Secretary, Canadian Section of the International
    Boundary Commission; Founding Member, Canadian Historical
    Association and the Board of Directors of the Canadian Writers
    Foundation; and Recipient, Medaille de Vermeil award from the
    Academie Francaise for his work in Canadian history and the Tyrrel
    Gold Medal from the Royal Society of Canada

Lawrence Johnstone Burpee was the eldest of six children born to Lewis
Johnstone Burpee and Alice Susannah DeMille.

Mr. Burpee married Maude Louise Hanington on June 29, 1899 in
Ottawa, Ontario, Canada. Lawrence and Maud had five children, three
sons and two daughters, over the space of the next fifteen years (Lawrence
Hanington, Ruth Maude, Margaret McLean Hanington, Edward Lewis
Hanington and Arthur DeMille Hanington).

He was educated partly at home and at public and private schools eventually obtaining his Doctorate of Laws degree from the University of Toronto in 1937. In 1890, he entered the Canadian Federal Civil Service to serve as private secretary to three successive Ministers of Justice. From 1905 to 1912 he was Librarian of the Carnegie Public Library in Ottawa. From 1912 until his death, he was Canadian Secretary of the International Joint Commission.

Burpee was one of the founding members of the Canadian Historical Association; National President of the Canadian Authors' Association; editor of the Canadian Geographical Journal; founding member of the Board of Directors of the Canadian Writers' Foundation; Fellow of the Royal Society of Canada (1911), Honorary Secretary (1926-1935), and President (1936-1937). He received the Medaille de Vermeil award from the Académie Française for work in Canadian history and the Tyrrell Gold Medal from the Royal Society of Canada.

Burpee published extensively in the areas of Canadian bibliography, geography and history. His publications include: A Bibliography of Canadian Fiction (1904, co-editor: L.E. Horning), Canadian Life in Town and Country (1905, co-author: H.J. Morgan), A Little Book of Canadian Essays (1909), A Century of Canadian Sonnets (1910), An Index and Dictionary of Canadian History (1911, co-editor: Arthur G. Doughty), Humour of the North (1912), Sandford Fleming, Empire Builder (1915), An Historical Atlas of Canada (1927, editor), Journals of LaVerendrye (1927, editor).

It was at the annual meeting of the Library Association in 1910 when Mr. Burpee began his "crusade", as Dolores Donnelly aptly called it, in her historical analysis *The National Library of Canada*. At the time, Lawrence was the chief of the Carnegie Library of Ottawa and incoming President of the Association. His speech to the delegates, later published in The University Magazine, lamented that Canada, like Abyssinia and Siam, had no national library. He proceeded to enumerate countries around the world that did. He borrowed his model of what a national library should be like from the Chief Librarian of the United States Congress, Herbert Putnam.

"It should have a collection universal in scope; it should have specialists to answer inquiries; and it should have an index of the collections of other libraries. Let the government adopt a policy of a national library."

He wanted it to be in a central location and have turned over to it books from the Library of Parliament that

"serve no very useful purpose in a pureful legislative library".

Visionary that he was, Mr. Burpee saw the national library being linked to the Public Archives, the Library of Parliament and government departments by a system of pneumatic tubes through which books and messages would be sent whizzing. Sixty years later, the Federal Government Library Survey returned to the matter, recommending not tubes but a delivery van

References:

Sketch of Lawrence Burpee by Wilfrid Flood, 1936
Burpee Family FTW, Internet Webpage
Census of Canada, 1881, 1901, 1911
Andrews Newspaper Index Cards, 1790-1976
England and Wales Death Index, 1984-2005
Canadian Solders of World War I, 1914-1918
Canadian Marriages, 1857-1924, Genealogical Research Library,
Find-A-Grave, Internet
Encyclopedia Canada, Vol. 2, p. 143; and the *Canadian Encyclopedia*, Page 242.
Photo of Lawrence Burpee, National Archives of Canada

LEWIS ARTHUR BURPEE

Born: March 29, 1887, Ottawa, Wellington, Ottawa, Ontario, Canada
Died: April 26, 1962, Ottawa, Wellington, Ottawa, Ontario, Canada
Buried: After April 26, 1962, Beechwood Cemetery, Ottawa, Ontario, Canada

Occupation: Business executive

Notable Accomplishment: President of Charles Olgilvy Limited, Ottawa, Canada

Lewis Arthur Burpee was the youngest of six children born to Lewis Johnstone Burpee and Alice Susannah DeMille. His father, Lewis Johnstone, is noted elsewhere in this book for his own accomplishments. With the exception of serving in the Canadian forces during World War I, Lewis Arthur was born, educated and lived in the New Edinburgh section of Ottawa, Canada.

Lewis A. Burpee married Lillian Agnes Orme on May 9, 1917 in Carleton, Ontario, Canada. Together, they raised five children during their marriage. The eldest child, Lewis Johnstone Burpee, will be described later in this book for his military service during World War II.

He joined the staff of Charles Olgilvy Limited in 1915 as secretary-treasurer. He was appointed Vice-President and General Manager of the department store in 1925. Upon the death of its founder, Charles Olgilvy, Mr. Burpee became President of the company and served in that capacity until his death. Under his leadership the company expanded and was known throughout Canada.

Mr. Burpee was instrumental in many civic organizations in Ottawa. He was one of the founders of the Community Chest of Ottawa and the Ottawa Credit Bureau. Also, he was the treasurer of the Union Mission for Men and was a former chairman of the Board of Trustees of the Royal Ottawa Sanatorium.

References:

Burpee Family, FTW, Internet Webpage
Canadian Soldiers of World War I, 1914-1918
Canadian Census: 1901
Genealogical Research Library, Canada Marriages, 1857-1924
Beechwood Cemetery Records, Ontario, Canada, 1873-1

LEWIS JOHNSTONE BURPEE

Born: March 15, 1918, Ontario, Canada
Died: May 17, 1943 Holland
Burial: Bergen Op Zoom War Cemetery, Bergen, Noord-Holland, Netherlands

Occupation: Pilot, Royal Canadian Air Force

Notable Accomplishment: Killed In Action, World War II, Dam Buster Project

Lewis Johnstone Burpee was born to Lewis Arthur Burpee and Lillian Agnes Orme. He was the second eldest of five children and was named after his grandfather who had the same name.

Lewis married Lillian Emma Westwood on September 10, 1942 in Southhampton, Hampshire, England. They had one child named after both his father and great-grandfather. Lewis Johnstone Burpee, III was born on December 24, 1943.

Pilot Officer Burpee was flying a Lancaster enroute to the Mohn Valley Dams. His plane, along with four other planes were lost on that day's mission. Their objective was to bomb the hydroelectric dams of the Ruhr Valley. The 617th squadron was to drop newly devised 9500 pound bombs at a height of 60 feet, about 450 yards from the dam, and at a speed of 230 miles per hour, the weapon would then skip along the water (and over any torpedo nets) until it struck the dam wall, the spinning maintaining the weapon's stability and slowing it down. The backward rotation would then cause the cylinder to roll down the dam wall where it would explode at a predetermined depth. The wall would be weakened and the great weight of water would cause the dam to collapse.

The men who took part in this air campaign were to be known as the "dam busters". As reported by The Nanton Lancaster Society and Flight Sargeant Ken Brown on that fateful day:

> "P/O Burpee was about a mile and a half off the north coast. They opened up on him and he blew up over the airport. So I knew we had one less."

Pilot Officer Burpee was awarded the Distinguished Flying Medal for his actions and sacrifice to the Allied Forces. This medal was given to his next of kin. The inscription for this award was:

> This airman has successfully completed a number of operational sorties against targets which include the naval ports of Wilhelmshaven, Bremen and Hamburg and also industrial centres in Italy. He has also participated in raids on Berlin, Nuremburg, and Stuttgart. He has constantly displayed the utmost determination to complete his allotted task, whatever hardships or dangers are encountered. From raids on Lorient and Saint Nazaire, he secured valuable photographs. Flight Sergeant Burpee has invariably exhibited coolness and courage and has performed his duties conscientiously and efficiently. In total, he flew twenty-six sorties of over two hundred and five hours.

References:

Burpee Family FTW, Internet Webpage
Ontario, Canada Deaths, 1869-1934
Veterans Affairs of Canada, Internet Webpage
London Gazette, Distinguished Service Flying Medal, May 18, 1943
All England and Wales, Marriage Index: 1916-2005

LUCIEN FRANCIS BURPEE

Born: October 12, 1855, Rockville, Tolland, Connecticut, USA
Died: May 9, 1924, West Hartford, Connecticut, USA
Buried: After May 9, 1924, Grove Hill Cemetery, Rockville, Tolland, Connecticut, USA

Occupation: Attorney and Judge

Notable Accomplishments: Major General, Connecticut National (Home) Guard 1917-1921; Judge, Connecticut Superior Court

Lucien Francis, son of Colonel Thomas Francis Burpee, was born in Rockville, Tolland County, Connecticut on October 12, 1855.

In 1863-64 he was for a time with his father and the regiment he commanded in Virginia, where his study was in Casey's tactics and his amusement in watching drills and parades. In 1874, he enlisted in the First Regiment, Connecticut National Guard, in Rockville, and was discharged in 1878 for non-residence.

In March, 1886, he was appointed second lieutenant of Company A, Second Regiment, Connecticut National Guard, in Waterbury, Connecticut; promoted to first lieutenant in June, 1886; to captain in June, 1887; to major in February, 1890; to lieutenant-colonel in May 1893; and to colonel in July, 1895; and held the command of his regiment until he retired in November, 1899. Under his command, this regiment was rated by USA army officers and assigned to inspect state organizations as one of the best drilled and disciplined in the country.

At the outbreak of the Spanish-American War, he recruited his regiment to the maximum strength allowed by law, and tendered it for service in the USA Volunteers, April 25, 1898, "for any time and in any place," and maintained it in fit condition and complete readiness for the field until the end of the war. In this offer and during this period, he was unanimously and heartily supported by all his officers and men; but their services not being immediately required, Colonel Burpee obtained temporary leave of absence from his command, and accepted a commission as lieutenant-colonel in the USA Volunteers, offered to him by President McKinley. He served with that rank during the campaign in Puerto Rico on the staff of Major General Nelson A. Miles, commanding USA army, and of Major General James H. Wilson, commanding First Division, First Army Corps. He was honorably mentioned for distinguished service.

After his return to the USA, General Wilson in his report said that Colonel Burpee 's conduct "reflected great credit on him, and that he was a man who would not have failed to reach the highest distinction had the war lasted." Colonel Lucien F. Burpee, a native of Waterbury, served as a judge advocate on General Nelson Miles' staff in postwar Puerto Rico. In October, 1898, Colonel Burpee was assigned to duty on the staff of General Wilson, who was then in command of the First Army Corps, and served in that position in Kentucky and Georgia until January 1, 1899. During that same period of time, he prosecuted American soldiers charged with burning the village of Coto, near Ponce. After obtaining five convictions, he was credited with positively influencing "the peace and quiet of the island, and the future relations of the people to the USA." Then, peace having been secured, he resigned and was honorably discharged.

Colonel Burpee was prepared in the public schools of Rockville to enter Yale College in 1875, and was graduated there with honors in 1879. He was a member of Phi Beta Kappa and of Skull and Bones, and editor of the Yale Record and of the Yale Literary Magazine. After graduation, he attended Yale Law School and Hamilton Law School, receiving his degree of LL. B. there in 1880. He then returned to Yale College for a year to take special work in American history and continue his studies in law. In 1881 he began to practice law in Waterbury in the office of the Hon. S.W. Kellogg, under the name first of Kellogg and Burpee, and afterwards of Kellogg, Burpee and Kellogg. This partnership was dissolved in 1889.

From 1883 to 1890 he was the prosecuting attorney of Waterbury; from 1890 to 1896 he was corporation counsel of the city; and from 1897 to 1909 he was judge of the Waterbury city court. In 1900 he took Terrence F. Carmody, of Waterbury, into partnership. In 1905 the office of judge of the district court of Waterbury was offered to him but he declined the position. In 1909 he was appointed a judge of the superior court of Connecticut, the highest trial court of the state.

Colonel Burpee had been active in public affairs, but never a candidate for office. He was a Congregationalist in religion; a member of Continental Lodge, No. 76, Free and Accepted Masons; of Nosahogan Lodge, Independent Order of Old Fellows; of Wadhams Camp, Sons of Veterans; of the Society of Foreign Wars; of the Military Order of the Loyal Legion of the USA; of the Spanish War Veterans; of the Society of the Porto Rican Expedition; of the Military and Naval Order of the Spanish War, and of the Sons of the American Revolution. He was awarded the medal given by Congress for foreign service in the Spanish-American War. He was a member of the Waterbury Club, of the Graduates and Union League clubs of New Haven, of the Army and Navy Club and of the USA Military Service Institution of New York.

He married (first) on September 25, 1881, Lida (Eliza) Wood, who was born April 25, 1860 and died July 23, 1889. She was a daughter of Stephen W. Wood, of Cornwall, New York, and Catherine C. B. (Ring) Wood, a descendant of James Sands, who settled in Plymouth, Massachusetts, in 1658, and in Block Island in 1661. He married (second) on August 2, 1894, Annie Morten Driggs, who was born April 4, 1866 in Waterbury, Connecticut. Ms. Driggs had been represented in an earlier law suit by Lucien Burpee. He married (third) on April 28, 1904, Irene A. Fitch who was born April 21, 1867 and died October 22, 1947, daughter of Martin P. and Exene (Tobey) Fitch, of Southfield, Massachusetts. She is a lineal descendant of Roger deKnapp, who was knighted by Henry VIII in 1540, and whose grandson, Nicholas, Mrs. Burpee 's ancestor, came with Governor Winthrop to Massachusetts in 1630.

Children by first wife, Lida Wood were: Lida and Helen (twins) were born August 31. 1883; Thomas Francis was born September 15, 1885 and Percival W was born (unknown).

There appear to be no recorded children by either the second or third wives.

References:

Lowell Daily Sun, Lowell, Massachusetts, August 2, 1894

Index of Connecticut Muster Roll for the Spanish-American War 1898-1904

Burpee, Lucien F., 19, 193

Record of Service of Connecticut Men In the Army, Navy & Marine Corps of the United States in the Spanish-American War, Philippine Insurrection, and China Relief Expedition from April 21, 1898 to July 4, 1904. Compiled by Authority of General Assembly under direction of Adjutant General, Hartford, Connecticut

The Story of Connecticut, by Charles W. Burpee, Volume II, Pages 824, 956, 958, and 967.

Genealogical and Family History of the State of Connecticut, Vol. I-IV

Connecticut in the War by Jonathan Ault

LUCY LIVERMORE BURPEE

Born: October 12, 1812, Sterling, Worcester, Massachusetts, USA
Died: August 19, 1888, Sterling, Worcester, Massachusetts, USA
Buried: After 19, 1888, Oak Hill Cemetery, Sterling, Worcester, Massachusetts, USA

Occupation: Housewife

Notable Accomplishment: Operator of Underground Railroad Safehouse (Runaway Slaves)

Lucy was the eldest of six children born to Newton Burpee and Myra Roper. She married General Uriel H. Tuttle on March 31, 1833 in Sterling, Worcester, Massachusetts. They, in turn, had ten children of their own between 1835 and 1854 (six females and 4 males).

Very little is known about her with the exception that Lucy and Uriel operated a safehouse in Torrington, Connecticut for the safe passage of slaves escaping to New England and Canada. While living in Litchfield County, Uriel Tuttle chaired the Connecticut Anti-Slavery Society, which eluded protesters by meeting in orchards, barns and sheds. Lucy and her husband fought slavery with a lecture series and the circulation of abolitionist literature.

The Tuttles established a depot at 3925 Torringford Street. In 1839, Uriel advanced his involvement by serving the manager of the American Anti-Slavery Society.

Reference:

The Underground Railroad: An Encyclopedia of People, Places and Operations by Mary Ellen Snodgrass, December 2007
Burpee Family, FTW, Internet Webpage
US Census: 1880
History of Slavery in Connecticut by Bernard Steiner, 1893

MARY ELISE BURPEE

Born: June 6, 1863, New London, Merrimack, New Hampshire, USA

Died: February 6, 1952, New London, Merrimack, New Hampshire, USA

Buried: After Feb 6, 1952, New London, Merrimack, New Hampshire, USA

Occupation: Housewife and Teacher

Notable Accomplishments: Taught at, and was later a College Trustee of, Colby-Sawyer College, New London, New Hampshire, USA; Served in the Red Cross during both World War I and II

Mary Elise Burpee was the second eldest of five children that Edwin Perley Burpee and Rosaline Parasine Todd raised in New London, Merrimack, New Hampshire. Mary Elsie was a fifth generation Burpee to live and work in New London, New Hampshire. Mary graduated from Colby College in 1885 and taught there for over a decade with a year break to attend Radcliffe College in Boston, Massachusetts. Later, she followed in the footsteps of her uncle (Anthony Colby Burpee) and grandfather (Perley Burpee) in serving as the first female college trustee for Colby-Sawyer College that is located in New London, New Hampshire. She served in this capacity for almost forty years.

Mary married Walter Leeds Macomber on September 1, 1897 in New London, New Hampshire. There are no recorded children from this marriage.

Mrs. Mary Burpee Macomber traveled extensively throughout the United States and abroad. In both World War I and World War II, she served her country by volunteering in the Red Cross.

References:

Burpee Family FTW, Internet Webpage
US Census: 1860, 1870, 1900
New York Passenger Lists, 1820-1957
The First Century of Colby by Henry K. Rowe, 1937, Page 398.

MOSES BURPEE

Born: August 11, 1750, Sterling, Worcester, Massachusetts, USA
Died: November 20, 1827, Sterling Worcester, Massachusetts, USA
Buried: After November 20, 1827, Chocksett Burial Ground, Sterling, Worcester, Massachusetts, USA

Occupation: Farmer and Reverend

Notable Accomplishment: Soldier, Revolutionary War, Battle of Lexington

Moses Burpee was the second eldest of nine children born to Jeremiah Burpee and Elizabeth Brocklebank. He, in turn, married Elizabeth Kendall on April 12, 1775 in Lancaster, Worcester, Massachusetts. They had seven children over a period of twenty years.

Moses served in the Revolutionary War as a corporal under Captain Thomas Gates' Company from Lancaster, on the Lexington Alarm of April 19, 1775 and Captain Solomon Stuart's Company under Colonel Josiah Whitney's Regiment on the Bennington Alarm of August 21, 1777.

His descendent Mrs. Mary Burpee Clark was successful in having his military actions recorded in the National Society of the Daughters of the American Revolution.

References:

Burpee Family. FTW, Internet Webpage
Inscriptions copied by Ruth Hopfmann and Barbara Dudley, 1983-1986
DAR Patriot Index, Volume 24, page 347, Number: 23993
The Military Annuals of Lancaster, Massachusetts, 1740-1865, Bennington Alarm, Page 163.

MOSES BURPEE

Born: February 25, 1847, Sheffield, Sunbury, York, New Brunswick, Canada
Died: August 18, 1936, Houlton, Aroostook, Maine, USA
Buried: Evergreen Cemetery, Houlton, Aroostook, Maine, USA

Occupation: Chief Engineer, Bangor and Aroostook Railway

Notable Accomplishment: Laid out the location and supervised the construction of the entire Bangor and Aroostook Railway

Moses Burpee was the son of George Burpee and Phoebe Elizabeth Burpee. He had five siblings. All six children were born in Sheffield, New Brunswick, Canada. Moses married Caroline Alexander on April 4, 1880 in Fredericton Junction, New Brunswick, Canada. They had two children: Mary Genevra and George William.

Moses received his early education in Sheffield, New Brunswick and his technical training in engineering from Franklin Institute, Philadelphia, 1866-1868. From 1870 to 1877, he was assistant engineer on location and construction of the European and North American Railway (now Maine Central). From 1877 to 1884, he was Assistant and Division Engineer for Canadian Pacific and Milwaukee Railways. In 1885, he was Chief Engineer of the New Brunswick Railway, and when this railroad was leased to the Canadian Pacific, he remained as Chief Engineer, Atlantic Division.

In 1891 he resigned and became Chief Engineer of Bangor & Aroostook Railway. He stayed on in this capacity until his death in 1936. In this capacity, he was credited with laying out the location and construction of the entire railroad.

References:

Maine Memory Network, Aroostook County Historical and Art Museum, Houlton, Maine
Canadian Census: 1861, 1871, 1891
US Census: 1910, 1920
New York Passenger Lists, 1820-1957
Burpee Family, FTW, Internet Webpage
The Houlton Resident Directory, 1895

NATHAN BURPEE

Born: December 12, 1758, Lancaster, Worcester, Massachusetts, USA
Died: January 5, 1836, Atlas, Genesee, Michigan, USA
Buried: After January 5, 1836, Perry-McFarlan Cemetery, Grand Blanc,
    Genesee, Michigan, USA

Occupation: Farmer

Notable Accomplishment: Private, Revolutionary War Soldier, Battle of
    Saratoga

Nathan Burpee was the son of Samuel Burpee, Jr. and Martha Brocklebank.
He was the oldest male sibling and one of ten children that Samuel and
Martha had during their marriage. Nathan was married twice. His first
wife was Eunice (Elizabeth) Farrar. They were married on November 28,
1782. Shortly thereafter, she passed away. His second wife was Lucinda
Pearson. They were married on April 8, 1787 in Sterling, Worcester,
Massachusetts. So after, there first of seven children was born. They had
five boys and 2 girls from 1788 through 1807.

Although many of Nathan's name sake took up the call of the American
Revolution, his is one of the better documented cases of his participation
in the Rebellion.

Nathan, initially served as a Private under Captain Goss in Colonel Ephraim Sawyer's Company. He marched through the Town of Hartford, Connecticut to a place called Horse-Neck and then onto Dobb's Ferry where he remained for about three weeks. Crossing the Hudson River into New Jersey he remained for about 2 days before recrossing the Hudson River.

On December 14, 1776, at the age of eighteen, he volunteered with his brother, Elijah, to serve in the militia for a term of three months in Town of Sterling, Massachusetts in a company commended by Captain Manasseh Sawyer. Within a fortnight, they marched to the Town of Dorchester, Massachusetts near Boston and mustered in Colonel Nicholas Dike's Regiment, until March 1, 1777. Nathan re-enlisted as a Private on September 3, 1777 in Captain William Greenleaf's Company of Colonel Job Cushing's regiment, soon after the Bennington Battle (August 16, 1777). They marched through New Salem, New York directly into Bennington, Vermont. Conditions were so dire that they had to kill their horses in Bennington, which were in a state of offensive putridity when they marched over the battlefield.

They marched to different points in advance of the British Army under General Burgoyne. In Bhemus (Bemis) Heights, the regiment that he was assigned to was equipped and paraded for action. They posted as a reserve expecting momentarily to be brought into action. Nathan witnessed the burying of the dead after the Battle of Bhemus (Bemis) Heights. After the surrender of Burgoyne at Stillwater, they marched down the North (Hudson) River and were onboard a sloop for one day and night.

Note: Battle of Bhemus(Bemis) Heights is commonly known as the second battle that took place at the Battle of Saratoga.

Thereafter, they marched for several days by land and encamped on frozen ground without tents, and finally arrived at a place called Horse-Neck, where he had been in 1776. They remained for a few days and drew provisions, then marched to Trenton, New Jersey where he was discharged on November 29, 1777 (age 19) after being there for a fortnight.

In July 1780 (age 21) he was a Private with Private Joseph Pearson in a Company commanded by Captain David Moore, with Lieutenants Houghton and Bailey. They marched from Worcester, Massachusetts through Newton to Bristol, Rhode Island, then crossed at Bristol Ferry and were stationed at Butts Hill where they were ordered to rebuild the fort that had been previously destroyed by the British.

Nathan was dismissed from the military on October 31, 1780. He always entered the service as a volunteer, except his first tour of duty of 2 months, when he was drafted into service. His pension (W.27391 BA-J/MLB) was $36.60 annually, starting March 4, 1834, and payable semi-annually on the 4th of March and the 4th of September of every year.

After the Revolutionary War, he resided for fourteen years in the Town of Chittenden, Vermont. He then moved to the Town of Hartford, and then Avon in Livingston County, New York, where he lived for 5 years. Thereafter Nathan moved to Wooster, Ohio and lived there for approximately twenty-six years and then back to Avon. Before 1835 (age 76), he moved from New York to Michigan with the intent of spending the remainder of his life with his children who moved from New York to Michigan. Shortly, thereafter, he passed away.

References:

Nathan Burpee's Revolutionary War Pension File #W27391
Sons of the American Revolution, Internet Data Base
Daughters of the American Revolution, DAR Society, 1994
Letter dated May 6, 1937, from the Veteran's Administration, Department of Revolutionary War Pensions, Washington, D.C.

NATHANIEL ADAMS BURPEE

Born: March 13, 1816, Grafton, Worcester, Massachusetts, USA
Died: December 11, 1887, Rockland, Knox, Maine, USA
Buried: After December 11, 1887, Achorn Cemetery, Rockport, Knox, Maine, USA

Occupation: Business Owner (Livery, Undertaker and Furniture)

Notable Accomplishment: State Senator, State of Maine

Nathaniel Adams Burpee was the eldest of seven children from the marriage of Heman Horton Burpee and Satira Redding. His father was a soldier in the 34th Massachusetts Infantry during the Civil War. Nathaniel married Mary Jane Partridge on December 27, 1838 in Rockland, Maine. They had five children between 1839 and 1851.

Nathaniel, and his brother Samuel, originally operated a livery/blacksmith business. This business had multiple carriages in which to transport larger items, often assisted families transporting the casketed remains of their deceased loved ones to the cemetery.

By 1830, Nathaniel and Samuel had started an undertakers business on the corner of Winter Street called *Burpee Undertakers*. Early funeral records show this business evolved to include washing, dressing and laying out (or casketing) which took place in the family home. Often the deceased individual was first placed on a draped Gleason Board, while the casket was constructed, lined and made ready. Eventually, they provided chairs for guests in the bereaved home, horse-drawn hearse for transfer to the cemetery and hacks in which the family and clergy rode. In 1872, Nathaniel's son, Edgar A. Burpee, joined the funeral business and was soon appointed President of Rockland's first funeral establishment. Edgar continued operation of the funeral and furniture business until selling to R.M. Leach, May 25, 1919. This undertakers business, funeral home, is still in business under the name of *Burpee, Carpenter and Hutchkins Funeral Home.*

Nathaniel was a decorator, painter and dealer in furniture. Overtime, he focused on the making of furniture. In 1835, he opened a furniture company in the Rockport area called N.A. and S.H. Burpee Furniture Company. This business flourished for many years with their furniture found throughout the Northeast.

As a successful businessman in Rockport and Rockland area, Nathaniel was active in his local community. Nathaniel was the first Chief Engineer of the Rockland Fire Department. In 1869, the N.A. Burpee hand engine was dedicated in his honor (see photo).

Eventually, Nathaniel turned his interests to politics. From 1857 to 1858, he was a Maine State Senator and in 1867 became the President of the State Senate. If this was not enough, he was musically inclined and served as a member of the Rockland Band for many years.

References:

Edmund West, comp.Family Data Collection—Births, database online, Provo, Utah: Ancestry.com, 2001

Brief History of the Rockland Fire Department, Internet Website, http://rocklandfd.com/history.php

Burpee Family, FTW, Internet Website

The History of Thomaston, Rockland and South Thomaston, Maine Volume 2, Pages 26, 165 and 349.

US Federal Census: 1850, 1880

Marriage Records of Lincoln County, Maine: To 1866, Page 80.

NATHANIEL BURPEE

Born: February 7, 1721/22, Rowley, Essex, Massachusetts, USA
Died: December 25, 1815, Candia, Rockingham, New Hampshire, USA
Buried: After December 25, 1815, Candia, Rockingham, New Hampshire, USA

Occupation: Deacon, Tailor, and Teacher of Singing

Notable Accomplishments: Early Settler of Candia, New Hampshire; Soldier in the French and Indian War (Siege of Cape Breton); Member, Committee of Inspection for Candia in the American Revolutionary War

Nathaniel Burpee was the youngest of three children of Jeremiah Burpee and Rebecca Jewett from Rowley, Essex, Massachusetts. Nathaniel fought at the Siege of Breton in the French and Indian War (1745). Nathaniel married Esther Rolfe on April 19, 1748 in Bradford, Essex, Massachusetts. Nathaniel and Esther had eight children from their marriage between 1750 and 1766.

In 1753, Nathaniel moved his family to Candia, New Hampshire. He taught signing to his student in his house. This music reportedly delighted their families. He was one of the first Deacons of his community church.

References:

History of Chester, New Hampshire, including Auburn: a supplement to the History of old Chester, published in 1869 (1926), Page 650.
HISTORY OF CANDIA: Once Known As Charmingfare; With Notice of Some of the Early Families, by F.B. Eaton, Press of the Granite Farmer, James O. Adams, Printer, Manchester, New Hampshire, published 1852, Page 56-57.
Vital Record of Rowley, Massachusetts to 1849, published by the Essex Institute, Salem, Massachusetts, 1928, Pages 39-40.
Burpee Family, FTW, Internet Webpage

NATHANIEL BURPEE

Born: February 19, 1753, Candia, Rockingham, New Hampshire, USA
Died: March 9, 1835, Candia, Rockingham, New Hampshire, USA
Buried: After March 9, 1835, Candia Hill Cemetery/First Cemetery,
    Candia, New Hampshire, USA

Occupation: Farmer

Notable Accomplishment: Soldier, American Revolutionary War

Nathaniel Burpee was one of six siblings from the family of Nathaniel
Burpee and Esther Rolfe. His father, by the same name, is referenced in
this publication as a soldier during the French and Indian Wars. Nathaniel
married Dorothy Currier prior to 1782 in an unknown location. From
1782 through 1792, Nathaniel and Dorothy had four children in Candia,
New Hampshire.

In November 1775, Nathaniel enlisted (#2505523) for two years as the
rank of private mostly under the direct command of Captain Moses Baker
who reported to regimental commander Lieutenant Colonel Joseph Welch.
Of those two years, he spent approximately two months at Cambridge
under the general command of General George Washington.

From September 27, 1777 to November 3, 1777, with the New Hampshire
volunteers, Nathaniel Burpee marched from Candia to join up with the
Northern Continental army at Saratoga and was present at the surrender
of British General John Burgoyne.

One of Nathaniel's officers, Lieutenant Abraham Fitts, who also marched with the volunteers, kept a diary in which he recorded his eye-witness and understated account of the surrender:

> "[October] ye 17 Friday Mr. Burgoyne marcht off the Ground; Genl Gates marcht In Then we marcht to Saratoge put up in a Barn"

As a footnote to this record, Nathaniel's brother (Nathan) served in the same regiment at the same time.

References:

American Genealogical-Biographical Index, Godfrey Memorial Library, Middletown, Connecticut, USA

New Hampshire Revolutionary War Burials, Internet Web Page, http://www.nhssar.org/NH%20Revolutionary%20War%20Burials.pdf

Burpee Family Tree, Internet Webpage

Sons of the American Revolution, Internet Database

DAR Patriot Index, Daughters of the American Revolution, Internet Database

Genealogy of Richard Currier of Salisbury and Amesbury, Massachusetts, (1616-1686): and many of his descendants, Page 45.

Saratoga National Historical Park, Internet Web Page, Reference #NH02, http://saratoganygenweb.com/batlbu.htm

PIERSON THURSTON KENDALL BURPEE

Born: January 2, 1829, Sterling, Worcester, Massachusetts, USA
Died: November 20, 1902, Sterling, Worcester, Massachusetts, USA
Buried: After November 20, 1902, Oak Hill Cemetery, Sterling, Worcester, Massachusetts, USA

Occupation: Mechanic

Notable Accomplishment: Lieutenant, U.S. Army, Civil War, Company K, 53rd Massachusetts Infantry Regiment

Pierson Thurston Kendall Burpee was the youngest of six children born to Nathan Burpee and Polly Gerry Jewett. Pierson married Julia Ann France Estabrook on October 25, 1855 in Sterling, Massachusetts. They had four children between 1857 and 1871.

Little is known about Pierson's life outside of his military career. At age 33, he enlisted as a 2nd Lieutenant on September 4, 1862 in Company K of the 53rd Massachusetts Infantry Regiment. He was promoted to 1st Lieutenant on November 18, 1862. The 53rd Regiment was comprised of volunteers from Princeton, Sterling, Lancaster,

Boylston, and New Braintree areas. This regiment served in, "The Army of the Gulf", seeing action primarily in and around Louisiana. Lieutenant Burpee was mustered out of service on September 2, 1863 in Groton, Massachusetts.

In an interesting twist of fate, Pierson's brother, Thomas Gerry Burpee, went South just prior to the outbreak of the Civil War and eventually married a woman from Georgia. As a result, his brother (Thomas Gerry Burpee) fought in the Confederate Army (Private, Civil War, Confederate, Georgia, 2nd Calvary, Company C). Indeed, as the saying goes brother fighting brother in this war.

References:

Burpee Family, FTW, Internet Webpage

U.S. Federal Census: 1850, 1870, 1880, 1900

Civil War Pension Index: General Index to Pension Files, 1861-1934

1890 Veterans Schedules, Database online. Sterling, Worcester, Massachusetts, ED 1047, roll 14, page 2.

U.S. Civil War Soldier Records and Profiles, Internet Database

Organization Index to Pension Files of Veterans Who Served Between 1861 and 1900, NARA Publication Number: T289

The Fitchburg Sentinel, Fitchburg, Worcester County, Massachusetts, November 21, 1902, Page 6.

53rd Regiment Massachusetts Volunteers by Henry A. Willis

RICHARD ALLEN BURPEE

Born: October 3, 1932, Delton, Barry, Michigan, USA
Died: Not Applicable At This Time
Buried: Not Applicable At This Time

Occupation: Air Force Pilot and General Officer

Notable Accomplishments: Lieutenant General, United States Air Force with last assignment as the Commander of Fifteenth Air Force; Chairman, Retired Officers' Association; and numerous military decorations

Richard Allen Burpee was one of eight children born to Harold D. Burpee and Gladys Estelle Hulst Renzema. Richard married Sally Dreve Fisher on June 11, 1966 in Bexar, Texas. Richard and Sally had two children, Richard and Brent, in 1969 and 1971.

Richard started his career in the United States Air Force by reporting for pilot training school at Lackland Air Force Base on December 3, 1953. Over the next four decades, he flew 11,000 hours, including 336 combat missions in Vietnam; commanded the 509th Bomb wing and the 19th Air division; commanded the Oklahoma City Air Logistics Center; served in the Air Force Headquarters at the Pentagon; served as the Director of Operations of the Joint Chiefs of Staff; and lastly, as Commander of the 15th Air Force with responsibilities for managing one half of the forces in Strategic Air Command. On January 1, 1986 he was promoted to Lieutenant General, United States Air Force.

In addition to these assignments, he was awarded the Defense Distinguished Service Medal, Air Force Distinguished Service Medal with cluster, Silver Star, Legion of Merit, Distinguished Flying Cross with cluster, Bronze Star and Air Medal with 14 oak clusters.

After retiring, Richard took on several civilian leadership positions in the State of Oklahoma. Among these positions were: Vice President of the University of Central Oklahoma and President of the Greater Oklahoma City Chamber of Commerce.

References:

Texas Marriage Collection, 1814-1909 and 1966-2002, Internet Data Base

Called to Serve: A General's Life Story by Lt. General Richard A. Burpee, Tate Publishing Enterprise, Mustang, Oklahoma, ISBN #978-1-60604-614-2

Email Correspondence, to/from Richard A. Burpee dated September 25, 2006

RICHARD E. BURPEE

Born: Abt. 1810, Douglas, York, New Brunswick, Canada
Died: February 26, 1853, Jacksonville, Duval, Florida, USA
Buried: After February 26, 1853, Unknown Location

Occupation: Merchant and Baptist Minister

Notable Accomplishment: First Canadian Missionary

Richard E. Burpee was the youngest of seven children of Thomas Lockwood Burpee and Esther Gallop. Richard married Laleah Johnstone on on April 5, 1845 in Wolfville, Kings, Nova Scotia, Canada. Richard and Laleah had four children between 1846 and 1853.

Richard E. Burpee became a general merchant in Fredericton. There he was converted and baptized on November 21, 1829, joining the Brunswick Street Baptist Church. Richard quickly became a leading member of that congregation, where he was greatly influenced by the ministry of the Reverend Frederick W. Miles, a keen advocate of foreign missions. Feeling himself called to the ministry, he was licensed to preach in 1836 or 1837. Then, on 7 September 7, 1837, he was ordained as the first minister of St George's Baptist Church (western branch).

As early as 1814 the Baptists of Nova Scotia and New Brunswick had expressed concern for "the poor heathen" in foreign lands. During the next two decades the Baptist denomination in the Maritimes grew significantly and so did interest in the oversea mission field. In June 1838 the Nova Scotia Baptist Association, "having taken into serious consideration the lamentable condition of the heathen world," asked its sister association in New Brunswick to join with it in "pledging themselves and the Churches to the adequate education and maintenance of a suitable person as a Missionary in some foreign field." The New Brunswick association warmly endorsed the proposal, and by the following year that "one suitable person" had been found.

Richard E. Burpee was twenty-nine years old when he responded to the appeal in 1839. The next year, in preparation for service overseas, he entered the newly established Queen's (after 1841 Acadia) College in Wolfville, Nova Scotia. Before graduating with a BA in 1844, he spent his summers fostering interest in the foreign missions throughout the Maritimes. By 1845 all the necessary arrangements had been made. Since the Baptists of the Maritimes did not have a mission station and could not afford one initially, it was arranged that Burpee and his wife would go as missionaries of the American Baptist Board of Foreign Missions, with Maritime Baptists committed to pay half of the expenses. After a very emotional farewell, the Burpees left Halifax on April 20, 1845, sailing to Burma via Boston.

The years in Burma, spent mostly at Mergui, among the Karens, were less successful than expected, although by 1848 Reverend Burpee had baptized his first converts. His health had begun to fail soon after his arrival and by 1849 he was forced to abandon the missionary enterprise. After his return to New Brunswick in 1850 his health continued to decline. He died three years later, probably of tuberculosis, in Florida, where he had gone for the climate.

However small his actual accomplishments in the mission field, to Maritime Baptists Burpee was the symbol of their brave new venture, the first of hundreds of such missionaries sent by that denomination. "Burpee" became a cherished, if unusual, Christian name given to generations of Baptist males. In addition, the desire to support Burpee and other Baptist mission endeavours was one of the most important factors bringing about, in 1846, the union of the New Brunswick and Nova Scotia Baptist associations to form the Baptist Convention of Nova Scotia, New Brunswick and Prince Edward Island (now the United Baptist Convention of the Atlantic Provinces).

References:

A HISTORY OF THE BAPTISTS by Thomas Armitage
Burpee Family Tree, Internet Data Base
The Acadia Record by Watson Kirkconnell, 1953
Dictionary of Canadian Biography Online, 1851-1860 (Volume VIII), Internet

ROBERT WILLIAM BURPEE

Born: August 5, 1941, Reading, Middlesex, Massachusetts, USA
Died: July 31, 2007, Miami, Dade, Florida, USA
Buried: September 29, 2007, Forest Glen Cemetery, Reading, Massachusetts, USA

Occupation: Meteorologist

Notable Accomplishment: Director, National Hurricane Center, Miami, Florida, USA

Robert William Burpee was one of four children that were born to William Edward Burpee and Thelma M McClintock.

He grew up in Reading and graduated from Reading Memorial High School in 1959. He played football, basketball and baseball in high school and served as president of his class. He graduated from Harvard University in 1963 and obtained his doctor of philosophy in meteorology from MIT in 1971.

Robert spent most of his career as a research scientist with the Hurricane Research Division of the National Oceanic and Atmospheric Administration. He was responsible for developing the program to fly hurricane hunter aircraft through hurricanes to obtain data and improve the accuracy of hurricane forecasting. He flew more than 265 flights that penetrated the eye walls of hurricanes.

The data now generated by hurricane hunter aircraft has produced a substantial improvement in the accuracy of predicting hurricane tracks. Max Mayfield, a former director of the National Hurricane Center in Miami recently stated that "Everyone living in hurricane-prone communities in the USA owes thanks to Bob Burpee for his tremendous contribution."

Dr. Burpee achieved a career-long dream in 1995 when he became the director of the National Hurricane Center. He served in that capacity from July 1995 until August 1997 when he had to step down for health reasons. During his tenure as director, he did not seek the spotlight. After retiring from his position as director, he remained active in hurricane research. He continued to write papers and speak at conferences.

His work in the field of hurricane research and safety is only equaled by Herb Saffir and Robert Simpson aka the Saffir-Simpson Hurricane Scale.

References:

Social Security Death Index, Database online. Number: 025-32-4398; Issue State: Massachusetts; Issue Date: 1959-1960.

ROYAL HUDDLESTON BURPEE, SR.

Born: 04 Jun 1897, New York, USA
Died: 13 Jan 1987, Easton, Northampton, Pennsylvania, USA
Buried: Long Island National Cemetery, Section 3F Site 2361, Farmingdale,
  Nassau, New York, USA

Occupation: Executive Director, United Services Organizations (USO) of
  the City of New York

Notable Accomplishment: Devised a physical aptitude test used by the
  United States Military and later for personal fitness

Royal Huddleston Burpee, Sr. was one of two children born to Burton
Lloyd Burpee, Sr. and Violet Rose Huddleston. Royal married Alvina Ella
Wintersohl on June 29, 1922. They, in turn, had two sons between 1924
and 1927.

Royal served in the United States Navy during World War I and as the
Overseas Program Director for the United Service Organizations (USO)
during World War II. Between his services to his country, Royal managed
to earn a doctorate degree in psychology from Columbia University in
June of 1930.

During the 1930's, Royal developed the *Burpee Test* for use by the United
States Military. Consisting of a series of the exercises performed in rapid

succession, the test was meant to measure agility and coordination. It is not clear whether the exercise itself was invented by him, or if his test merely popularized it. This exercise continues to be used throughout the country for personal fitness. It is now commonly called *The Burpee.*

In September of 1946, Dr. Burpee was appointed as the Executive Director of the Bronx-Union Branch of the New York City Young Men's Christian Association (YMCA). He retired from this position in 1964. Royal continued to be affiliated with the Greater New York YMCA until his death.

References:

Oxford Dictionaries, Internet Webpage, http://oxforddictionaries.com/definition/burpee

U.S. Federal Census: 1900, 1910, 1920, 1930

Social Security Death Index, Database online. Number: 099-26-8378; Issue State: New York; Issue Date: 1951.

U.S. Veterans Gravesites, New York.1775-2006, Internet Webpage, http://search.ancestry.com/cgi-bin/sse.dll?db=vacemeteries&h=480786&indiv=try

World War I Draft Registration Cards, 1917-1918, Internet Webpage, http://search.ancestry.com/cgi-bin/sse.dll?db=ww1draft&h=2415643&indiv=try

New York Times, Columbia University Graduation, June 3, 1930

New York Times, Appointment to the YMCA, September 5, 1946

The Morning Call, Obituary, January 14, 1987

THOMAS BURPEE

Born: September 3, 1639, Birkby, Yorkshire, England
Died: 01 Jun 1701, Rowley, Essex, Massachusetts, USA
Buried: After June 1, 1701, Rowley, Essex, Massachusetts, USA

Occupation: Watchman and Weaver

Notable Accomplishment: First known Burpee in America

Thomas Burpee is largely thought to be the first Burpee to immigrate to America. What is known about him is subject to scrutiny concerning its accuracy. That being said, the following is generally accepted about this individual.

Thomas Burpee was the son of Thomas Burpee (aka: Birkby, Birkbe, Birkee,) and Beatrice Webster. It is believed that he arrived in the Boston area around 1635. He reportedly had moved to Rowley, Massachusetts by January 30, 1647. He applied his knowledge of weaving (that he had learned in England) to support himself in Rowley.

Thomas married his first wife, Martha Cheney, on June 14, 1653 in Rowley, Massachusetts. They had three children between 1654 and 1658 (Hannah, John, and Sarah). After the death of Martha, Thomas married his second wife, Sarah Kelley, on April 15, 1659 in Rowley, Massachusetts. They, in turn, had three children between 1660 and 1675 (Sarah, Thomas, and Mary).

Thomas conveyed the following to his son Thomas, approximately ten years prior to his passing in a document dated December 20, 1690:

> "The moiety or halfe part of all his housings, buildings, Orchard, upland ground, tillage land & pafture, marsh or meadow ground enclofed wilderness Lands lying Scituate & being in ye confines of Rowley" together with half of all his "quick stock or living creatures" Thomas, junior, to maintain his parents during their lives and to pay his sisters, Sarah

Spofford and Mary, 20 pounds each, and his niece (parent's granddaughter), Hannah Higgins, 5 pounds.

References:

Pioneers of Massachusetts by Charles H. Pope, Page 80.
The Early Records of the Town of Rowley, Massachusetts, Page XI.
The Burpee Family of Essex County by Dr. Frank A. Gardner, Pages 67-69.
Burpee Family, FTW, Internet Webpage
Massachusetts Vital Record to 1850, New England Genealogical Society, Page 449

THOMAS FRANCIS BURPEE

Born: February 17, 1830, Stafford, Tolland, Connecticut, USA
Died: June 11, 1864, White House, Virginia, USA
Buried: After June 11, 1864, Grove Hill Cemetery, Section 2, Rockville,
　　Hartford, Connecticut, USA

Occupation: Foreman, Woolen Cloth Mill

Notable Accomplishment: Colonel, Civil War, Union, 21st Regiment,
　　Connecticut Volunteers

Thomas Francis Burpee was the youngest of seven children from the marriage of Thomas Burpee and Betsey Temple. Thomas Francis Burpee married Adeline Minerva Harwood November 28, 1852 in Stafford, Connecticut. Thomas and Adaline had two children (Lucien Francis and Charles Winslow) between 1855 and 1859. Both of these children are profiled in the book based on their own prominence.

In 1849, he joined the 4th Company, 5th Regiment of Infantry, Connecticut State Militia. He later met Adeline, and they were wed on Thanksgiving Day in 1852. Thomas was working as an operator in the Hockamm Woolen Mills when his first son, Lucien, was born in 1852. A second son, Charles, arrived in 1859, by which time Thomas was working at the Windermere Mill in Ellington.

As rumors of war with the South moved through his peaceful Connecticut community, Thomas prepared for the possibility of conflict. Over the years he had attained the rank of captain with the militia, and when President Lincoln called for troops in April 1861, Captain Burpee offered his well-drilled company for service in the volunteer army. Lincoln's appeal, however, had been met with such response that Burpee's offer was declined. Ironically, the men's assistance was not accepted, but their guns and accoutrements were: their materiel was confiscated due to the sharp shortage of arms and equipment.

Then, as the war progressed, the need for more troops was realized. Lincoln requested an additional 300,000 men for three year's service, and Captain Burpee and his men were ready. On July 12, 1862, Captain Burpee was given command of Company D, 14th Connecticut Infantry, a unit comprised, in part, of many of his friends from state militia units.

Due to his many years of military service and the urgent need for experienced officers, Captain Burpee was offered the position of major in the 21st Connecticut. Initially he declined, stating his wishes to stay with his friends in the 14th. However, Governor Buckingham's entreaties to him eventually had their desired effect, and Thomas became major of the 21st on August 23, 1862. He was soon promoted to lieutenant colonel of the regiment, under the command of West Point graduate Colonel Arthur H. Dutton.

In his many letters to Adeline, Thomas gives us a glimpse into the heart of a soldier, a patriot, and a Christian. In his first letter, written from Camp Kearny in Washington and dated September 15, 1862, he noted, "The battalion behaves very well indeed for raw troops, it is made up of good men." Several days later, a disappointed Burpee wrote: "We are, I am told, to constitute a corps of reserves, which is not so pleasing to us when we hear of glories being won by our brothers in arms."

From the first he had a solemn appreciation of his situation. From Camp Pleasant Valley, Maryland, on October 12, 1862, he wrote:

> 'Tell them [the relatives] that I consider it a very great privilege to be called a soldier of the Republic, and that I hope to have that privilege until the monster rebellion is crushed out, utterly and forever, until they who have dared lay their

desecrating hands upon the flag of our Union shall be made
to bite the dust.'

Around January 1863, Lt. Colonel Burpee came down with rheumatic
fever and was granted a twenty-day leave of absence. His condition did not
improve until the end of April, when he rejoined his regiment. On June
7, the 21st Connecticut's surgeon requested that Lt. Colonel Burpee be
granted a minimum of thirty days leave, which he felt was "indispensable
to prevent death of permanent disability." Thomas returned home, where
he made a slow recovery, then returned to the regiment yet again on
August 31, 1863.

In late summer 1863, the 21st was transferred with their division (Getty's)
to the Department of Virginia and North Carolina. Through late 1863
and spring 1864, they remained in the Suffolk, Virginia, area in relatively
quiet possession of the territory.

In early May 1864, Thomas and his men participated in the Bermuda
Hundred Campaign as past of Gen. Brooks' Division. On May 16, 1864,
the 21st Connecticut, with Lt. Colonel Burpee in command and Colonel
Dutton as brigade commander, was engaged at the Battle of Dewry's Bluff.
The battle was hard-fought, and on May 17 Burpee wrote to Adeline:

> 'The rebels got reinforcement the day before. The night had
> been foggy and wet, and at four o'clock the fog was so thick
> that nothing could be seen two rods off. I had just sent out
> Captain Brown with his company in front of the Twenty-First
> as skirmishers when a tremendous firing opened on the right
> of my brigade, which was the right of the whole line occupied
> by our troops. The enemy had turned our right flank and were
> in our rear. The Ninth New Jersey and the Twenty-Third and
> Twenty-Seventh Massachusetts were almost used up by the
> suddenness of the attack.
>
> I will not attempt to describe the whole fight. Suffice it
> to say that in an hour and a half I was left alone with the
> Twenty-First to cope with the enemy who were in my front
> and both flanks, and a thick swampy woods in my rear. The

men fought well, in some cases hand to hand with the rebs. I changed my front to rear and fought for five hours through the swamp and timbers, gradually falling back, sometimes charging upon them when they pressed too hard on us, and at last succeeded in bringing the regiment and most of my wounded on to the open grounds, where I could get help. Our Brigadier—General was captured and I received no orders at all until I had fought three hours, and when the fight commenced I could not tell how things were going on my right, and did not know the enemy had got around us until their bullets came from that direction. I don't know what the generals at headquarters think of the conduct, but I hear that we have gained much credit. We were so long in the woods that they thought we should be captured . . . I lost one hundred and six men and four commissioned officers. As for myself, I received no scratch, A bullet struck the spur on my heel and glanced off. God covered my head in the danger and brought Maine safely through.'

Burpee's concerns were both those of a commanding officer and a family man, on May 22, 1864, he wrote to Adeline,

"I received yours of the sixteenth this morning with joy. You say 'go! And God be with you!' May God bless you my darling wife, for that! It gives Maine unspeakable joy to know that you are resigned to leave everything in the hands of God and trust him for the results! . . . When in battle my only constant prayer was God bless my dear wife and children,"

General Grant ordered the 18th Corp to reinforce the Army of the Potomac and toward the end of May they moved down the James River and up the York River to White House Landing. From there the men marched to Cold Harbor, and on June 3, 1864, the 21st Connecticut was in the thick of the attack there. Commanded once again by Lt. Colonel Burpee, the 21st attacked the Confederate position and was under heavy fire not 200 yards from the enemy for three hours. The regiment was ordered to rely on their bayonets and prepared to charge, but the order was countermanded when the great force of the enemy was seen. The regiment's losses were forty-seven killed or wounded. After the Battle of Cold Harbor, Thomas wrote to Adeline from the trenches:

> "It is appointed unto men once to die; and it matters little when or where, if we are prepared and engaged in duty."

It was his last letter to Adeline. At daybreak on the morning of June 9, 1864, while inspecting the skirmish lines as brigade officer of the day, Colonel Burpee was wounded in the chest by a sharpshooter's bullet. Unknown to him, he had been promoted to colonel of the 21st on the previous day.

Colonel Burpee was removed to White House Landing, where he was placed in the 18th Corps Hospital. The regimental chaplain, Thomas G. Brown, joined the colonel soon after he was wounded. On June 17, 1864, Chaplain Brown wrote to Mrs. Burpee:

> 'I was with him in the ambulance during the night on his way from the front to the White House . . . I had the melancholy task to inform him that the doctors said he could not live.
>
> I asked if he had any directions to give you in relation to his affairs, after a pause he said to Maine "Chaplain, don't you leave Maine till you meet my friends"; I told him I would not. I asked him how he felt, he said his trust and confidence was in God and his greatest regret was to die without seeing you and his children. On the afternoon of Saturday [June 11] I prayed with him, he wanted to sit up, and when I laid him down with a heavenly smile on his countenance he said, "Bless the Lord."
>
> What I have in my possession is his watch which he wished you to have, and his saber to his eldest son. I sincerely mourn with you for I loved him as a brother and as a Mason he was doubly dear to Maine. He was dear to the regiment also. They feel his death very much.

Colonel Burpee's body was embalmed and sent by express via Washington to Rockville, Connecticut. He was put to rest in Grove Hill Cemetery on June 12, 1864, the major of the 21st Connecticut Infantry, Hiram B—Crosby, wrote in his report:

> 'Lt. Colonel Burpee had borne his part with distinguished valor all during the Bermuda Hundred Campaign. His coolness and good judgment at the Battle of Drewrys Bluff will not soon be forgotten by his comrades in that hard contested action. At Cold Harbor he was equally conspicuous for gallantry. While in command of the regiment he was able and efficient, always discharging with promptitude every duty, particularly if concerning the comfort and welfare of his men, by whom he was much loved and respected.'

On July 15, 1864, by order or Maj. Gen. B.F. Butler, General Order No.80 was issued in memory of officers killed in the Bermuda Campaign. Battery No.8 was named Battery Burpee in honor of Colonel Thomas Francis Burpee.

In post-war correspondence written by Governor Buckingham on October 2, 1866, to Colonel Thayer, a friend of Burpee's, the governor eulogized Col. Burpee:

> 'my kind regards to Mrs. Burpee and say that from the time her honored husband entered the service to this hour I have never entertained any other than high respect for his ability and fidelity as an officer as well as for his personal character; that he is one of the few officers against whom I never heard a complaint. I sympathize with her in her affliction, but doubt not that so pure an offering, presented in the name of human liberty upon the altar of our country, is accepted by Him who said that "Inasmuch as ye have done it unto one of the least of these my brethren, ye have done it unto Maine."'

Gov. Buckingham then penned the line that would be engraved on the monument Mrs. Burpee commissioned for the colonel's gravesite in Grove Hill Cemetery, Rockville:

'In the hour of national peril he gave his life to his county, leaving this testimony-that he was a pure patriot, a faithful soldier and a sincere Christian.'

In May 1887, Lucien, Colonel Burpee's older son, responded to a request that he attend the 21st Connecticut Volunteer Infantry's reunion:

'I most sincerely regret that I must lose the honor and pleasure of meeting the brave men whom my father loved so well and led so often into danger. It is one of the proudest thoughts in my experience that I am the son of a man who for himself as the commander of a famous fighting regiment in the late rebellion won the esteem and admiration or them all, from highest to lowest.

On the wall of my library hang a sword and belt-battered, worn and blood-stained. Whatever my success in life may be, these mementos of your comrade's scarifice and death will be the richest gift I can bestow upon my children.'

In May of 1884, the Grand Army Post #71 was chartered in Rockville, Connecticut. They took the name of Burpee Post in the memory of Colonel Thomas Francis Burpee, Commander of the 21st Connecticut Volunteer Infantry.

References:

A Compendium of the War of the Rebellion by L. Dyer, 1959.
National Archives, The Official Records of the War of the Rebellion, various volumes, 1891.
The Story of the Twenty-First Regiment Connecticut Volunteer Infantry compiled by members of the regiment, Sewart Printing, Middletown, Connecticut, 1900.
History of New London County, Connecticut, With Biographical Sketches Of Many Of Its Pioneers And Prominent Men by Duane Hamilton Hurd, J.W. Lewis and Company, 1882
Burpee Family, FTW, Internet Webpage

New England Civil War Museum

U.S Federal Census: 1860

Military Records of Individual Civil War Soldiers, Data compiled by Historical Data Systems of Kingston, Massachusetts http://www.ancestry.com/search/rectype/military/cwrd/db.htm

Willimantic Journal June 24, 1864, page 176

Organization Index to Pension Files of Veterans Who Served Between 1861 and 1900,

National Archives and Records Administration

WASHINGTON ATLEE BURPEE

Born: May 5, 1858, Sheffield, Sunbury, York, New Brunswick, Canada
Died: November 26, 1915, Fordhook Farm, Doylestown, Bucks,
    Pennsylvania, USA
Buried: After November 26, 1915, Doylestown Cemetery, Plot: Section
    M, Plot 49, Bucks, Pennsylvania, USA

Occupation: Business Owner

Notable Accomplishment: Founder of the W. Atlee Burpee Seed Company

Washington Atlee Burpee was the eldest of three children of Dr. David
Burpee III and Ann Katherine Kate Atlee. Washington married Blanche
T. Simmons on April 30, 1892 in Philadelphia, Pennsylvania. Washington
and Blanche had three children (David, Washington Atlee Jr., and Stuart
Alexander) between 1893 and 1901.

Washington Atlee was expected to become a physician like his prominent
father (in Philadelphia, Pennsylvania) and grandfather (in New Brunswick,
Canada), but even in his early youth he seemed determined to pursue a
different career. His boyhood hobby was poultry breeding—an interest
that soon expanded to include the breeding of livestock, dogs, and plants.
The infant science of genetics fascinated him.

At fourteen, Atlee was already actively breeding chickens, geese and turkeys. By the time he was in his mid-teens, he was corresponding with English breeders, providing as well as receiving information, and gained quick recognition when his papers on his experiments were published in England. The English breeders must have been impressed. That on one occasion, in fact, several of these eminent breeders came to the Burpee home, expecting to exchange information with a gentleman of some maturity—and therefore mistaking Dr. Burpee for his son. They were astonished to learn that the breeding expert they sought was 16 years old! Soon afterward, yielding to his father's wishes, he enrolled at the University of Pennsylvania Medical School, but he disliked it and simply could not visualize himself as a surgeon. When he dropped out, his father was predictably angry, but his mother was more tolerant of her son's unconventional interest and ambition.

In 1876, an 18-year-old Atlee started a mail-order chicken business out of the family home with $1,000 (equal to $20,556 today) loaned to him by his mother and a partner. Poultry farmers from the Northeast already knew of his talents, and he soon opened a store in Philadelphia, selling poultry and also corn seed for poultry feed. It wasn't long before his customers started requesting cabbage, carrot, cauliflower and cucumber seeds. In 1878, Burpee dropped his partner and founded W. Atlee Burpee & Company. The company soon switched to primarily garden seed, but live poultry wasn't dropped from the Burpee catalog until the 1940s.

By 1888, the family home, Fordhook Farm in Doylestown, Pennsylvania was established as an experimental farm to test and evaluate new varieties of vegetables and flowers, and to produce seeds. Before World War I, Atlee spent many summers traveling through Europe and the United States, visiting farms and searching for the best flowers and vegetables.

Atlee shipped many of the vegetables and flowers he found to Fordhook Farms for testing. Those plants that survived were bred with healthier types to produce hybrids better suited to the United States. Fordhook Farms was the first laboratory to research and test seeds in this way. Fordhook Farms specialized in testing onions, beets, carrots, peas and cabbage. Largely as a result of this work, Burpee became a household name, and the largest seed company in the world by the 1890s.

At the time of his passing, the Burpee Seed Company was sending out a million catalogs a year to customers.

References:

Wikipedia, Internet Database

The Legacy of W. Atlee Burpee, Internet Webpage, 2011, *http://www.burpee. com/gardening/content/the-legacy-of-w.-atlee-burpee/legacy.html*

Biography & Genealogy Master Index (BGMI), Gale Research Company. Biography and Genealogy Master Index. Detroit: Gale Research Co., 2005

Burpee Family, FTW, Internet Database

U.S. Federal Census: 1900, 1910

WILFRED E. BURPEE.

WILFRED ERNEST BURPEE

Born: 07 Feb 1860, New London, Merrimack, New Hampshire, USA
Died: 29 Apr 1948, Manchester, Hillsborough, New Hampshire, USA
Buried: After April 29, 1948, Village Cemetery, New London, Merrimack,
    New Hampshire, USA

Occupation: Optometrist

Notable Accomplishment: Partner, Brown & Burpee; College Trustee,
    Colby-Sawyer College

Wilfred Ernest Burpee was the eldest of five children born to Edwin Perley Burpee and Rosaline Parasine Todd (sister of Governor Anthony Colby). Wilfred married Lucy Nelson Shepard November 28, 1894 in Manchester, New Hampshire. Wilfred and Lucy had two daughters (Milfred Shepard and Helen) between 1896 and 1901.

Wilfred worked for several years as the owner of the summer hotel *The Heidelburg* before going in 1891 to the Detroit Optical College receiving the degree of optical specialist. Upon returning to Manchester he joined the well know optometrist firm of Brown and Burpee. The Brown and Burpee business specialized in optical defects and artificial eyes. In addition to his professional work, Wilfred was a trustee of the Colby-Sawyer College of New London, New Hampshire. He took great pride in this responsibility as it had been passed down from his father and grandfather.

In an interesting footnote discovered by the New Hampshire Medical Board in recent years, Wilfred was the first individual to have his license revoked by the State of New Hampshire. The revocation, on January 13, 1898, was apparently based on a revised evaluation of his credentials which showed him to be an "oculist" rather than a medical doctor.

References:

Burpee Family, FTW, Internet Webpage

American Genealogical-Biographical Index, Godfrey Memorial Library, Middletown, Connecticut

U.S. Federal Census: 1860, 1870, 1900, 1910, 1920, 1930

The First Century of Colby by Henry K Rowe, copyright 1937, Pages 245 and 398.

Personal Written Correspondence, housed by Colby-Sawyer College, New London, New Hampshire

Willey's semi-centennial book of Manchester, 1846-1896 by George Franklyn Willey, 1896, Page 87.

New Hampshire Board of Medicine, Newsletter, Volume 1, Issue 8, August 1998 https://www.nh.gov/medicine/publications/documents/vol1iss8898.pd

New Hampshire Medical Licensure Book, January 1898

WILLIAM PARTRIDGE BURPEE

Born: April 13, 1846, Rockland, Knox, Maine, USA
Died: December 15, 1940, Rockland, Knox, Maine, USA
Buried: After December 15, 1940, Unknown, Assumed, Rockland, Knox, Maine, USA

Occupation: American Marine Impressionist (Artist)

Notable Accomplishment: Bronze Medal, Pastels, 1904 Saint Louis Exposition (World's Fair)

William Partridge Burpee was one of five children from the marriage of Nathaniel Adams Burpee and Mary Jane Partridge. William's father, Nathaniel Adams, is detailed within the confines of this book. William never married and had no children.

As a young man he was educated in Rockland schools and in the Kents Hill Academy in Readfield, Maine.

After briefly advertising himself as an artist in the Rockland City Directory in 1882, Burpee appeared that year in Boston. By September 1, 1885, he was painting figures on Lynn Beach, Massachusetts, between Nahant and Swampscott in a style that now reflected the influence of French painting—particularly Eugene Boudin and Emile Louis Vernier. He showed life of the beach with children at play, dorymen, lobstermen, netmenders, women waiting for the return of the boats, clamdiggers, and drying and folding sails. He began exhibiting in Boston in 1881 (Massachusetts Charitable Mechanics Association) and soon became a regular exhibitor

(1890) and a member (1894) of the Boston Art Club. Until his trip abroad, Burpee maintained a position in bookkeeping and accounting.

In 1897, Burpee left Boston to tour Spain, Italy, France and England. He returned to the United States in 1899 and the next year returned to spend the summer in Holland. After his international travel and visits to the salons in Paris he became much more international in his viewpoint and his style became much more impressionistic. During the summer in Holland, he discovered pastel and soon developed a great facility and liking for the medium.

He was honored at the St. Louis Exposition of 1904 with a bronze medal for pastel. He also exhibited at the Pennsylvania Academy of Fine Arts, the Art Institute of Chicago, the Corcoran Gallery, Washington D.C., the American Watercolor Society, the L. D. M. Sweat Museum (now Portland Museum of Art), the Boston Society of Watercolor Painters and the Copley Society, Boston.

William is last listed with a Boston address in 1913. He reappears in Rockland in 1914 and is listed as dividing his time from 1927-1933 between Rockland and East Orange, New Jersey.

His work is in the permanent collections of the Museum of Fine Arts, Springfield, Massachusetts, the Rockland Public Library, Cheekwood, Nashville, Tennessee, Columbia Museum of Art, Columbia, S.C., the Louisiana State University Museum of Art, the William A. Farnsworth Museum, Rockland, Maine, and the Portland Museum of Art, Maine.

References:

Childs Gallery, Internet Webpage, http://www.childsgallery.com/artist bio.php?artist_id=67
U.S. Federal Census: 1850, 1880, 1910, 1930
Burpee Family, FTW, Internet Webpage
Biography and Genealogy Master Index, Gale Research Company, Detroit: Gale Research Company, 2005
U.S. Passport Applications, 1795 to 1925, Generations Network, Inc., 2007